T0344170

PREPARE

WORKBOOK WITH DIGITAL PACK

Caroline Cooke
Catherine Smith

Second Edition

A2

LEVEL 2

Cambridge University Press
www.cambridge.org/elt

Cambridge Assessment English
www.cambridgeenglish.org

Information on this title: www.cambridge.org/9781009023078

© Cambridge University Press and Cambridge Assessment 2015, 2019, 2021

First published 2015
Second Edition 2019
Second Edition update 2021

20 19 18 17 16 15 14 13 12 11 10 9 8

Printed in Malaysia by Vivar Printing

A catalogue record for this publication is available from the British Library

ISBN 978-1-009-02307-8 Workbook with Digital Pack
ISBN 978-1-009-02306-1 Student's Book with eBook
ISBN 978-1-009-03208-7 Teacher's Book with Digital Pack

CONTENTS

>> GET STARTED!

VOCABULARY   Things in the classroom

1 Complete the words with the missing vowels.

0 p_e_nc_i_l c_a_s_e_

1 d _ _ _ r
2 c _ _ m p _ _ t _ _ r
3 b _ _ _ r d
4 _ _ x _ _ r c _ _ s _ _ b _ _ _ k
5 c h _ _ _ r

6 b _ _ g
7 c _ _ _ t
8 p _ _ n s
9 t _ _ _ c h _ _ r
10 r _ l _ r
11 r _ _ b b _ _ r

12 m _ _ p
13 t _ _ x t b _ _ _ k
14 w _ _ n d _ _ w
15 p _ _ s t _ _ r

2 Which things in Exercise 1 are in your bag?

pencil case,

3 Find 12 things from Exercise 1 in the picture. Write them below.

1 ....   **4** ....   **7** ....   **10** ....
2 ....   **5** ....   **8** ....   **11** ....
3 ....   **6** ....   **9** ....   **12** ....

4 Which word doesn't belong in each group?

0 rubber   pencil case   pens   chair
_____chair_____

1 chair   board   door   teacher
....

2 map   poster   window   computer
....

3 pen   coat   rubber   ruler
....

4 board   computer   exercise book   window
....

5 bag   window   door   chair
....

GRAMMAR   Verb _be_

1 Are the sentences right (✓) or wrong (✗) for you? Correct the wrong sentences.

0 My pencil case is black and white. ☒
My pencil case is blue.

1 The chairs in my classroom are green. ☐
....

2 The classroom door is white. ☐
....

3 The board is green. ☐
....

4 My coat is brown. ☐
....

5 My bag is blue and yellow. ☐
....

there is / there are

2 Complete the questions with *Is there* or *Are there*.

0 _____Are there_____ any pens in your pencil case?
1 _____ any windows near your desk?
2 _____ a computer on the teacher's desk?
3 _____ a rubber in your pencil case?
4 _____ any maps on the walls in your classroom?
5 _____ a door near the board in your classroom?
6 _____ a coat on your chair?

3 Answer the questions in Exercise 2 for you.

0 *Yes, there are. There are two pens in my pencil case.*
1 ....
2 ....
3 ....
4 ....
5 ....
6 ....

have got

4 Choose the correct form of the verbs to complete the sentences.

0 My mum *have got* / *(has got)* a white bag.
1 I *have got* / *has got* two bottles of water on my desk.
2 My friends *haven't got* / *hasn't got* any money today.
3 This room *haven't got* / *hasn't got* any windows.
4 We *have got* / *has got* some posters on the walls.
5 I *haven't got* / *hasn't got* an exercise book.
6 You *haven't got* / *hasn't got* your textbook here today.
7 She *have got* / *has got* a computer at home.
8 The teacher *haven't got* / *hasn't got* a coat today.

5 Put the words in the correct order to make questions.

0 you / got / have / phone / a / ?
Have you got a phone?
1 got / have / friends / your / pens / ?
....
2 your / computer / dad / has / a / got / ?
....
3 friend / best / have / got / you / a / ?
....
4 teacher / a / has / your / got / coat / blue / ?
....
5 you / have / pet / a / got / ?
....

6 Answer the questions in Exercise 5 for you.

0 *Yes, I have.*
1 ....
2 ....
3 ....
4 ....
5 ....

7 What have you got in your bag? Use the words in the box or your own ideas.

textbook	exercise book	football
bottle of water	pencil case	
money	phone	food

In my bag I've got …

....
....
....
....
....
....

1 Write the numbers.

0	7	*seven*
0	*9*	nine
1	14	
2		eighteen
3	20	
4		twenty-three
5	31	
6		forty
7	56	
8		sixty-two
9	71	
10		eighty-five
11	90	
12		a hundred

Dates

2 Put the letters in the correct order to make months.

0	A i l p r	*April*
1	b e e e m p r S t	
2	l J u y	
3	a c h M r	
4	A g s t u u	
5	a M y	
6	b c D e e e m r	
7	e J n u	
8	a a J n r u y	
9	b c e O o r t	
10	a b e F r r u y	
11	b e e m N o r v	

3 Write the months in Exercise 2 in the correct order.

0	*January*	6	
1		7	
2		8	
3		9	
4		10	
5		11	

4 Write the dates.

0	11/11	*11th November*
1	16/09	
2	30/06	
3	07/10	
4	23/02	
5	13/12	
6	21/08	

5 Answer the questions and write the dates.

0 When's your teacher's birthday?
His birthday is on 21st March.

1 What's today's date?

2 When's your best friend's birthday?

3 What date is the first day of school?

4 What's tomorrow's date?

5 When's the next school holiday?

1 Match the verbs to the words and phrases.

0	draw	*c*	a	a bike
1	make		b	a cake
2	play		c	a tree
3	ride		d	three languages
4	run		e	tennis
5	speak		f	on your head
6	stand		g	underwater
7	swim		h	5 km

2 Write questions with the phrases in Exercise 1.

0 *Can you draw a tree?*
1 ....
2 ....
3 ....
4 ....
5 ....
6 ....
7 ....

3 Answer the questions in Exercise 2 for you.

0 *Yes, I can.*
1 ....
2 ....
3 ....
4 ....
5 ....
6 ....
7 ....

4 Complete the sentences with the phrases in Exercise 1 or use your own ideas.

0 I _____can ride a bike_____ but I can't
_____stand on my head_____ .
1 I .... but I can't
....
2 My mum can ....
but she can't ....
3 My friends can ....
but they can't ....

Present simple

5 Complete the text with the present simple form of the verbs in brackets.

Hi, my name is Jack. I⁰ *have got* (have got) a brother and a sister. I¹ .... (like) music and I² .... (love) travelling. Ravi and Molly are my friends. Ravi³ .... (not have got) any brothers or sisters and Molly⁴ .... (have got) one sister. Ravi⁵ .... (like) all sports and he⁶ .... (play) football every day. Molly ⁷ .... (not play) football. She⁸ .... (like) swimming.

6 Put the words in the correct order to make questions.

1 books / what / like / you / do / ?
....
2 you / do / pictures / like / drawing / ?
....
3 school / what / do / sports / play / you / at / ?
....
4 watching / like / you / do / TV / ?
....
5 animal / what / favourite / your / is / ?
....

7 Answer the questions in Exercise 6 for you.

1 ....
2 ....
3 ....
4 ....
5 ....

8 Complete the sentences for you.

1 Hello, my ....
2 I've got ....
3 I like .... and
I love ....

WRITING   A text about your best friend

1 Match the questions to the answers.

1 How old are you?
2 What's your address?
3 What's your phone number?
4 Have you got any brothers or sisters?
5 Who's your favourite pop star?
6 What's your favourite school subject?

a Yes, I've got two sisters.
b It's 13 Green Road.
c It's Rihanna.
d I'm 13.
e I love maths.
f It's 477888.

2 Write about your best friend. Use the questions in Exercise 1 to help you and write about 50 words.

My best friend is ....
....
....
....
....
....
....
....
....
....
....

1 SPORTS AND GAMES

VOCABULARY Sports

1 Match the words in the box to the photos.

| athletics | badminton | baseball | cycling | gymnastics | hockey | ~~rugby~~ |
| sailing | skating | snowboarding | surfing | table tennis | volleyball |

0 _____rugby_____

1 _____

2 _____

3 _____

4 _____

5 _____

6 _____

7 _____

8 _____

9 _____

10 _____

11 _____

12 _____

2 Complete the table with the sports in Exercise 1.

play	go	do

3 Choose the correct verbs to complete the sentences.

0 My sister (plays) / goes volleyball at the weekend.

1 My friends John and Toby play / go sailing in the summer.

2 We go / do athletics in the evening.

3 My brother plays / goes hockey on Sundays.

4 I don't play / go table tennis with my friends.

5 Do you play / go snowboarding alone?

1 Put the adverbs of frequency in the correct place on the line.

always	never	often	sometimes	usually

0% ————————————————————————— 100%

1 _____ 2 _____ 3 _____ 4 _____ 5 _always_

2 Rewrite the sentences with the adverbs of frequency in brackets in the correct place.

0 I watch sport on TV. (never)
  I never watch sport on TV.

1 My sister goes cycling with my dad. (usually)

2 I play rugby with my friends. (never)

3 Snowboarding is dangerous. (sometimes)

4 My friends do gymnastics after school. (often)

5 My grandparents play table tennis on Sundays. (always)

3 Put the words in the correct order to make questions.

0 do / play / often / you / baseball / ?
  Do you often play baseball?

1 you / in the city / usually / go / cycling / do / ?

2 badminton / parents / play / often / do / your / ?

3 you / go / often / do / snowboarding / how / ?

4 friends / your / rugby / school / do / play / sometimes / at / ?

5 do / go / always / sailing / you / in the summer / ?

4 Answer the questions in Exercise 3 for you.

0 _No, I don't. I never play baseball._
1 _____
2 _____
3 _____
4 _____
5 _____

5 Correct the mistakes in the sentences.

0 At school, usually we play volleyball on Friday.
  At school, we usually play volleyball on Friday.
1 I go swimming always on a Sunday.

2 I often am tired in the evening.

3 People go sometimes cycling with their friends.

4 At the weekend, usually I do sports.

5 In the holidays, we go sometimes sailing.

VOCABULARY   Sports equipment

1 Find nine more words for sports equipment and sports.

a	b	e	s	g	b	h	k	b	d	i
f	o	o	t	b	a	l	l	n	p	l
e	a	c	i	d	t	r	u	g	b	y
i	r	a	c	k	e	t	m	y	a	g
g	d	a	k	f	b	e	g	s	l	c
m	r	h	p	r	t	n	h	d	l	i
h	o	c	k	e	y	n	a	o	c	e
c	b	s	u	r	f	i	n	g	n	f
l	d	k	e	f	a	s	u	n	f	b

2 Choose the correct words to complete the sentences.

1 Hockey players hit the ball with a *stick / bat*.
2 You use a small white *board / ball* when you play table tennis.
3 Tennis *balls / rackets* are usually yellow.
4 Baseball players hit the ball with a long *stick / bat*.
5 In badminton, players use a *racket / stick* to hit the ball.
6 When you go surfing, you use a *ball / board*.

1 Read the text about Lola. How often does she do her favourite sport?

Teenblog: Sport

It's hard work, but it's fun!
Posted by Lola O'Shea

At school, I do a lot of sports like rugby, badminton and hockey. I love football, but now I have a new favourite sport – underwater football! Do you know it? It's like football, but you play it in a swimming pool. There are two teams. Each team has got 13 players, with five players in the water. The ball isn't a normal football; it's big and heavy. In normal football, players don't use their hands to hit the ball, but in underwater football, they can use their head, hands or feet to do this. Players try to hit the ball into the other team's goal. The winning team is the team with the most goals at the end of the game.

I don't play underwater football at school, but I'm in a team at a club. We usually play every week, on Saturday. Underwater football is an exciting sport but it's hard work. I love it because I like football and I like swimming, too. It's really fun!

2 Read the text again and choose the correct answers.

1 What sports does Lola do at school?
  A rugby, badminton and underwater football
  B rugby, badminton and hockey
  C rugby, badminton and swimming
2 How is underwater football different to normal football?
  A There are three teams.
  B The players use a racket to hit the ball.
  C You play it in a swimming pool.
3 How do you win a game?
  A You swim to the other team's goal.
  B You score goals.
  C You hit the ball.
4 Why does Lola like underwater football?
  A because it's exciting and fun
  B because she's in a team
  C because it's hard work

3 Read the text again and complete the table.

Underwater football facts

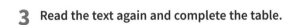

Number of teams	1	
Number of players in each team	2	
Equipment	3	
What do you use to hit the ball?	4	

LISTENING

🔊 01 1 Listen to an interview with teen sports star, Andrea Murray. Tick (✓) the activities that Andrea does regularly.

plays volleyball ....
plays tennis ....
goes snowboarding ....
cycles ....
studies ....
listens to music ....
reads ....
goes to the cinema ....

🔊 01 2 Listen to the interview again. Are the sentences right (✓) or wrong (✗)?

1 Andrea listens to Barry's podcast. ....
2 Andrea's father plays badminton. ....
3 Andrea's brothers and sisters don't
  like sport. ....
4 Andrea always plays tennis on school
  days. ....
5 She gets up at five o'clock on Wednesdays. ....
6 She doesn't have any free time. ....

🔊 01 3 Listen again and complete Andrea's diary.

Friday

- 5.00 am – ⁰ _get up_
- ¹ .... for
  two hours
- go to school

Saturday

- ² .... – get up
- have breakfast
- ³ .... all day

Sunday

- 6.00 am – get up
- morning – ⁴ ....
- afternoon – ⁵ ....

WRITING — A text about your favourite sport

1 Read the text. Tick (✓) the questions that the writer answers.

1 What is your favourite sport? ....
2 How do you play it? ....
3 What equipment do you need? ....
4 Where and when do you play it? ....
5 Why do you like it? ....

My favourite sport
by Lydia

My faborite sport is basketball. Does you know it? There are to teams with five people in a team. You need a basketball and two baskets to play it. Players throw the bal in the net two score points. The team with the most points wins. I sometime play basketball at school, but I also in a team at a club. We playing every Saturday. I like basketball becase it's fast and its fun.

2 Read the text again and find ten mistakes with spelling and grammar.

3 Think about your favourite sport and answer the questions in Exercise 1. Make notes below.

....
....
....

4 Write about your favourite sport. Use the notes you made in Exercise 3 and write about 50 words. Remember to read your work carefully and check for spelling and grammar mistakes.

....
....
....
....
....
....

2 THIS IS MY DAY

VOCABULARY — Daily routines

1 Complete the phrases with the verbs in the box.

brush	check	~~clean~~	get
have	leave	prepare	
put	tidy	wake	

0 _clean_ your teeth
1 _____ your room
2 _____ the house
3 _____ up
4 _____ breakfast
5 _____ your messages
6 _____ dressed
7 _____ your school bag
8 _____ on your shoes
9 _____ your hair

3 Complete the text with the correct form of phrases in Exercise 1.

Hi, I'm Keisha and this is my morning routine. On school days, I usually ⁰ _wake up_ at 7 o'clock. Before I get out of bed, I ¹ _____ on my phone. Then, I ² _____ in the kitchen with my parents. I usually have fruit, biscuits or bread, but I don't really like breakfast. I ³ _____ in my room. I usually wear jeans and a T-shirt. Then, I ⁴ _____ (I do this at least twice a day and after every meal!) and brush my hair. After, I ⁵ _____: I take my homework, books, lunch and my phone – that's very important! Then, I put on my shoes and ⁶ _____ at 8 o'clock. I always walk to school with my friend Lucas.

2 Match the phrases in Exercise 1 to the photos.

1 _____

2 _____

3 _____

4 _____

5 _____

6 _____

7 _____

8 _____

9 _____

10 _____

GRAMMAR — Present continuous and present simple

1 Look at the example sentences a and b. Then complete the rules below with the phrases in the box.

a I always leave the house at 8 o'clock.
b I'm wearing a T-shirt and jeans today.

> adverbs of frequency   present continuous
> present simple   *today*, *now* and *at the moment*

We use the ¹ _____ to talk about habits and routines. We often use it with ² _____.

We use the ³ _____ to talk about things we're doing now. We often use it with words like ⁴ _____.

2 Choose the correct words or phrases to complete the sentences.

1 I *always / at the moment* prepare my school bag before school.
2 My parents *now / always* watch TV in the evening.
3 My brother is making breakfast *now / usually*.
4 Why have you got your maths book? We're studying English *often / today*.
5 What are you doing *sometimes / at the moment*?
6 I don't *usually / never* go to bed at 9 o'clock.

3 Complete the sentences with the present simple or present continuous form of the verbs in brackets.

0 He _____plays_____ (play) tennis every day.
1 I never _____ (tidy) my room. My mum hates it!
2 They usually _____ (watch) films at the weekend.
3 My dad _____ (cook) breakfast today.
4 My mum _____ (not work) in a school. She's a police officer.
5 Jack _____ (not work) today because he's not very well.
6 What book _____ (you / read) at the moment? Is it good?

4 Correct the mistakes in the sentences.

1 I study now because I've got an exam tomorrow.
_____
2 Are you knowing Katy? She's my sister.
_____
3 My brother watching TV with his friends.
_____
4 My mum is a doctor. She is usually working at weekends.
_____
5 Every day we are drinking tea for breakfast.
_____

VOCABULARY — Food

1 Look at the photos and choose the correct words.

1 We eat *cereal / rice*, *bread / pasta* and *jam / honey* for breakfast.

2 In summer, we often have salad with *cabbage / cheese* and *tomatoes / cucumber* for lunch.

3 Yesterday I ate *fish / meat*, *rice / pasta* and *mango / vegetables*.

4 I usually eat *fruit / yoghurt* for dessert.

2 Match the words to the meanings.

1 breakfast   **a** the large part of a meal
2 dessert   **b** a drink, usually made from fruit
3 dinner   **c** the first meal of the day
4 juice   **d** you eat this between meals
5 lunch   **e** you eat this in the evening
6 main course   **f** you eat this at midday
7 snack   **g** you eat this sweet food at the end of a meal

3 Complete the sentences for you.

1 For breakfast, I always have _____.
2 My favourite dessert is _____.
3 My favourite snacks are _____.
4 For dinner, we usually have _____.

1 Read the texts. For each question, write *A* (Anna), *L* (Lena) or *Y* (Yuko).

1 Who has a hot drink in the morning? ....
2 Who uses the computer in the evening? ....
3 Who goes to school by bus or car? ....
4 Who does sport in the afternoon? ....
5 Who can't choose what she wears to school? ....
6 Who goes home before 2 pm? ....
7 Who takes her lunch to school? ....

My school day

Anna – the USA

I always get up at 6.30 am. Breakfast is cereal and milk. After breakfast, I prepare my school bag and leave the house at 7.30 am. I usually go to school on the school bus, but sometimes my mom drives me. Lessons start at 8.00 am every day. I have lunch at school. My dad makes a cold lunch for me every morning. I usually have sandwiches and fruit. School ends at 2.30 pm and I catch the school bus home. In the evening, I do my homework and watch TV.

Lena – Germany

I get up at 6.00 am and leave the house at 7.00 am. I always walk with my friend Grete. School starts at 7.30 am. We have five or six lessons every day. They finish at 1.30 pm and I usually go home for lunch. I sometimes go to homework club after school. We have dinner at 7.00 pm, and then I often watch videos on the internet.

Yuko – Japan

I get up at 7.30 am and have breakfast with my sisters. It's usually rice or eggs with tea. I put on my uniform, and then I leave the house at 8.15 am and walk to school. Lessons start at 8.30 am. Students all have lunch at school – fish and rice with vegetables. School finishes at 3.00 pm, and I have volleyball or badminton clubs after lessons every day. I leave school at 5.00 pm and go home. In the evening, I go to music lessons and do my homework.

2 Read the texts again and answer the questions.

1 What does Anna have for breakfast?

2 How does Yuko travel to school?

3 What time does school start for Lena?

4 What does Anna usually have for lunch?

5 What does Lena do after dinner?

6 When does Yuko do her homework?

LISTENING

1 Listen to the conversation between Jasmine and George. Where are they?

....

2 Listen again. Who says what? Write 'J' (Jasmine) or 'G' (George).

1 I'm shopping for my parents. ....
2 I thought you always play football on Saturday afternoon. ....
3 There isn't any football today. ....
4 Well, actually, I love chips too. ....
5 I like chocolate, but I don't eat it often. ....
6 I never eat chocolate. ....

3 Listen again and choose the correct answers.

1 Jasmine's mum is *working / on holiday* at the moment.
2 The people in the football team are *at home / on holiday*.
3 George's sister wants to *make eggs / go to university*.
4 George's sister wants to have lunch at *1.15 / 1.30* pm.
5 Jasmine wants to buy *biscuits / chocolate*.
6 Jasmine's dad *likes / doesn't like* chocolate.

WRITING — A paragraph about your routine

1 Read the text and match the times to the activities.

A typical school day
– by Leo

I get up at 7 o'clock and get dressed. My breakfast is cereal or toast. Then I prepare my school bag and go to school at 8 o'clock. I usually walk to school but sometimes I go on the bus. School starts at half past eight and finishes at 3 o'clock. Lunch is at 1 o'clock. I usually have sandwiches or a salad. After school I go home. Dinner is at half past seven. After dinner, I do my homework and go on the internet. I go to bed at half past nine.

1 7.00 am ....   a have dinner
2 8.00 am ....   b go home
3 8.30 am ....   c go to bed
4 1.00 pm ....   d get dressed
5 3.00 pm ....   e leave the house
6 7.30 pm ....   f start school
7 9.30 pm ....   g have lunch

2 Look at the text again. Find and <u>underline</u> sentences with *and*, *but* and *or*. Then complete the rules with *and*, *but* and *or*.

1 We use .... to link two ideas.
2 We use .... to contrast two things.
3 We use .... for different things we can choose.

3 Complete the sentences with *and*, *but* and *or*.

1 I walk to school with my friends Ally .... Hamish.
2 Do you go to school at 8 o'clock .... at 8.30?
3 For breakfast, I have cereal, ... I don't have toast.
4 I have tea .... hot chocolate. I don't have both.
5 I like football, ... I don't like basketball.
6 In the evening, I do my homework .... then I watch TV.

4 Think about the activities you do in a typical day and what time you do them. Use the ideas in Exercise 1 and your own ideas. Make notes below.

....
....
....

....

5 Write a paragraph about a typical school day. Use the notes you made in Exercise 4 and write about 50 words. Remember to use *and*, *but* and *or* in your text.

....
....
....
....
....
....
....
....

3 GREAT SOUNDS

VOCABULARY Music

1 Put the letters in the correct order to make words for types of music.

0 o p p   *pop*
1 p a r
2 e o p r a
3 c o r k
4 p i h – p o h
5 z a z j
6 c l l a a c i s s   u m i s c
7 l u s o

2 Match the words in the box to the photos.

> drums   electric guitar   keyboard
> piano   saxophone   violin

3 Match the definitions to the words.

1 This musical instrument is big. Some parts of it are black and white. It doesn't use electricity.
....

2 This is a type of music. The singer says the words quickly. ....

3 This is a type of music. The singers sing every word. You usually listen to it in a theatre. ....

4 You use your mouth and hands to play this musical instrument. ....

5 You hit this musical instrument with your hands or sticks. ....

a rap
b drums
c piano
d opera
e saxophone

1 ....

2 ....

3 ....

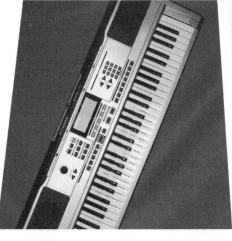

4 ....

5 ....

6 ....

GRAMMAR *like, don't like, hate, love + -ing*

1 Number the sentences in order 1 (☺) to 4 (☹).

a I hate learning English.
b I like learning English.
c I don't like learning English.
d I love learning English.

2 Complete the sentences with the correct form of the verbs in brackets.

1 I love _____ (write) stories.
2 My friends don't like _____ (run).
3 I hate _____ (catch) the bus to school.
4 My family loves _____ (make) pizza.
5 My brother likes _____ (practise) the electric guitar.
6 I like _____ (swim) in the sea.

3 Write the sentences with the correct form of the verbs.

0 My mum / love / cook
  My mum loves cooking.
1 My brother / not like / do / homework
  _____
2 I / hate / play / the piano
  _____
3 My sister / love / rap
  _____
4 My best friend / like / read / books
  _____
5 My dad / like / play / the violin
  _____

4 Correct the mistakes in the sentences.

👁 1 I like go shopping at weekends.
  _____
2 He doesn't like to watching opera on TV.
  _____
3 I don't like play football at school.
  _____
4 She love reading books.
  _____
5 We love listen to music.
  _____

VOCABULARY Music phrases

1 Choose the correct words or phrases.

1 become *famous / on stage*
2 give *a concert / in a band*
3 play *famous / in a band*
4 become *a singer / concert*
5 go *on tour / an album*
6 teach *a concert / music*
7 record *famous / an album*
8 make *a music video / on tour*

2 Complete the sentences with the correct form of the verbs in Exercise 1.

1 My history teacher _____ in a rock band.
2 My sister wants to _____ famous.
3 My mother _____ music to children in a school in Barcelona. Her students love her!
4 Tamara doesn't want to _____ a singer. She wants to play the drums.
5 Does your cousin want to _____ an album with her band?
6 My friends have a band and like _____ concerts for their families.
7 My brother loves singing. He wants to _____ a music video.
8 Holly loves travelling and she _____ on tour with her band every summer.

3 Complete the text with the words in the box.

rock	musician	instruments
keyboard	actor	record	festival

My best friend at school wanted to become an ¹ _____ and work in the theatre or on television. But I just wanted to play in a band. I wanted to give lots of concerts and ² _____ hundreds of albums!
I first got a guitar when I was about ten. I was quite good at playing that, but then started to play the ³ _____ when I was older, too. I liked that more. Mum plays the piano and Dad plays five different ⁴ _____ ! We sometimes practise all together. We all like listening to ⁵ _____ music but we often listen to classical music too.
Now, I'm in a band with three of my friends and we're becoming famous. Last week, we played at a music ⁶ _____ and on a TV show, and there are lots of photos of us on the internet. I love being a ⁷ _____ !

1 Read the text about a famous theatre school.
What kind of people study at the school?

A famous theatre school

Do you love singing, acting or dancing? At a theatre school, young people learn how to become actors, dancers and singers. There are many theatre schools in the UK. One of the most famous is the Sylvia Young Theatre School in London. Children aged between 10 and 16 go there. There are about 250 students at the school. Famous students from the past include the singers Leona Lewis and Dua Lipa.

At the Sylvia Young Theatre School students study the same subjects as students at other secondary schools, like maths, history and science. Students also take the normal school exams at 16. They do these school lessons on Mondays, Tuesdays and Wednesdays. Then they do dancing, singing or acting classes on Thursdays and Fridays. There aren't any lessons on Saturdays or Sundays. You can also study at the Sylvia Young Theatre School in the holidays, and they do classes for adults, too.

2 Read the text again. Are the sentences right (✓) or wrong (✗)?

1 There aren't many theatre schools in the UK.
2 There are 350 students at the Sylvia Young Theatre School.
3 Twelve-year-old children can study at the Sylvia Young Theatre School.
4 Students study maths at the Sylvia Young Theatre School.
5 Students learn how to sing, dance and act on Saturdays.

3 Read the text again and answer the questions.

1 Where is the Sylvia Young Theatre School?

2 Who are some famous students from the school?

3 When do students study normal school subjects?

4 What do students do on Thursdays and Fridays?

LISTENING

🔊 03 **1** Listen to the conversation between Sam and a music teacher. What instrument does Sam want to learn?

_____

🔊 03 **2** Listen again and complete Sam's notes.

MUSIC LESSONS

Time of lessons:	⁰ _4_ o'clock
Days of lessons:	¹ _____ and Fridays
Price of lessons:	² £ _____ an hour (for two lessons a week)
Address:	18 East Road – near the ³ _____
Teacher's name:	Mrs ⁴ _____
Teacher's phone number:	⁵ _____

WRITING   A text about music and you

1 Read the text and answer the questions.

1 What are Kate's favourite types of music?

2 Who are her favourite singers?

3 What musical instrument does she play?

Music and me

My name's Kate and I'm 13 years old. My friends and I all like listening to music. I think pop and hip-hop are exciting but jazz is boring. My favourite singer is Beyoncé. She's a really good singer. I also like Taylor Swift. Her music is great.

I listen to music at home and it's fun, but I love playing music, too. I'm in a band called The Pink Elephants! I play the electric guitar. It's great!

2 Look at the text again and underline the words *and*, *also* and *too.*

3 Complete the sentences with *and* and *also*.

1 I think rap is great. I _____ like hip-hop.
2 My sister likes listening to pop music. She _____ plays the saxophone.
3 He plays in a band _____ he sings.
4 Shakira is a good singer _____ she's a great dancer.
5 Her music is exciting. She _____ gives a lot of concerts.
6 My favourite singer is Ed Sheeran. I _____ like Bruno Mars.

4 Answer the questions in Exercise 1 for you. Make notes below.

_____

_____

5 Write about music and you. Use the notes you made in Exercise 4 and write about 50 words. Remember to use *and*, *also* and *too*.

_____

_____

_____

_____

_____

_____

4 IT WAS AWESOME!

VOCABULARY Adjectives

1 Complete the words with the missing vowels to make adjectives.

0 _a_ w _e_ s _o_ m _e_
1 __ m __ z __ ng
2 w __ n d __ r f __ l
3 f __ n __
4 t __ r r __ b l __
5 r __ __ lly g __ __ __ d
6 __ K

7 f __ nt __ st __ c
8 gr __ __ __ t
9 h __ rr __ bl __
10 b r __ ll __ __ __ n t
11 l __ v __ ly
12 p __ r f __ c t

2 Complete the table with the words in Exercise 1.

very, very good	all right	very bad
awesome		

3 Choose the correct words to complete the sentences.

1 Your new mobile phone is *brilliant / horrible*. I want to get one.
2 I love my new shoes. They're *fine / awesome*!
3 This food is *lovely / terrible*. I can't eat it.
4 The book I'm reading is *OK / perfect*. It's not good or bad.
5 That was a *horrible / wonderful* test. It was very difficult.
6 You got top marks for your essay. It was *fine / really good*!

GRAMMAR   Past simple of *be*

1 Rewrite the sentences in the past simple.

0 It isn't fun.
It wasn't fun.

1 We aren't at school.

2 It's very cold.

3 I'm at a party.

4 She isn't at the park.

5 Is he at home?

6 You're very happy.

2 Choose the correct words to complete the sentences.

1 I *was / were* at the park with my family yesterday. We like going there.

2 **A:** Why *wasn't / weren't* you at school yesterday?
B: I wasn't well.

3 **A:** *Was / Were* you at Sam's party on Saturday?
B: Yes, I *wasn't / was*.

4 He *was / wasn't* my teacher last year but he is this year.

5 The weather *was / wasn't* great last week – really sunny!

6 We *wasn't / weren't* at home on Monday afternoon. We always play football in the park on Mondays.

3 Complete the conversation with *was*, *were*, *wasn't* and *weren't*.

Izzy: Hey, Ben, where ⁰ _____were_____ you on Saturday? You ¹ _____ at football club.
Ben: I ² _____ at my mum's 40th birthday party.
Izzy: ³ _____ it fun?
Ben: Yes, everyone from my family ⁴ _____ there. Mum ⁵ _____ really happy.
Izzy: ⁶ _____ your family from Australia there, too?
Ben: Yes, they ⁷ _____. The weather ⁸ _____ very good for a party – it was cold and rainy, but we ⁹ _____ inside the house. It ¹⁰ _____ a really great day.

4 Correct the mistakes in the sentences.

👁 **1** Where was you yesterday?

2 Yesterday, it is sunny.

3 I very happy because the test was easy.

4 We are at the beach last weekend.

5 The film was starts at 4 o'clock.

6 My parents was at a party on Saturday night.

VOCABULARY   Emotions

1 Find ten adjectives for emotions in the wordsnake.

worriedupsetinterestedsorryhappynervousgladafraidsurprisedangry

| 1 | 2 | 3 | 4 | 5 |
| 6 | 7 | 8 | 9 | 10 |

2 Choose the correct words to complete the sentences.

1 I'm *sorry / worried* I'm late. The bus was full.

2 I'm *afraid / interested* of big dogs. I don't like them.

3 The teacher was *happy / angry* because my homework was excellent.

4 I've got a big test at school today. I feel a bit *upset / nervous*.

5 My brother is in hospital and I feel *upset / interested*.

6 After school, I tidied the house and did my homework. My dad was very *interested / surprised*.

READING

1 Read the three reviews of special days and match them to the photos.

A

bungee jumping

B

a trip in a hot-air balloon

C

a day at a theme park

1 _____

An awesome trip!

It was my birthday last month, and this was my best present. I am interested in flying, so it was a wonderful experience. Before the trip, I was a bit nervous, but everything was great. The weather was lovely and the views were amazing. I was surprised because it was very quiet. As soon as we were down, I wanted to go up in the balloon again. *Freddie*

2 _____

Just terrible!

I was on holiday with my friends and they were all interested in this. I was nervous and afraid, but there was no time to think! After the jump, I was really upset, but glad that I was back on the ground. It was a horrible experience. *Josh*

3 _____

A great day!

This was a special day with my family for my mum's birthday. Before the trip, I was worried because a lot of theme parks are for small children, but this place was brilliant. It's perfect for teenagers and adults! I love swimming, so the water slides were really fun. It was fantastic! I can't wait to go again! *Maddy*

2 Read the reviews again and choose the correct answers.

1 The weather on Freddie's trip was *good / bad*.
2 Freddie *was / wasn't* happy after his special day.
3 Josh was *surprised / worried* about his jump.
4 The experience for Josh was *good / bad*.
5 Maddy *didn't like / liked* the theme park.
6 Maddy *doesn't want / wants* to repeat the special day.

3 Find words in the text to match the meanings.

Freddie's review
1 what you can see from a place ....

Freddie's review
2 with no sound, not noisy ....

Josh's review
3 terrible ....

Maddy's review
4 people over 18 years old ....

1 Listen to five short conversations. For each question, choose the correct picture.

1 Where was Olivia on Saturday?

2 What was the weather like at the theme park?

3 Where were Joni's parents last weekend?

4 When was Amy's birthday?

5 Who was at the swimming pool?

WRITING A description of a special day

1 Read the text and look at the questions. Which question does the writer not answer?

1 Which day of the week was the special day?
2 Who were you with?
3 What was it like?
4 Where was it?
5 What time was it?

My special day – Morgan

Last weekend was very special because I was at a concert on Sunday night. It was my favourite singer – Ariana Grande. The tickets were quite expensive, but it was a present for my birthday. I was there with my two best friends, Emma and Lucas. The concert was at 9 o'clock, and I was very tired at school on Monday. But I was glad I was at the concert. It was fantastic!

2 Read the text again and find adjectives to describe the things.

1 the weekend
2 the tickets
3 Morgan's feeling on Monday morning
4 the concert

3 Think about a special day you had, for example, a trip to a theme park, a camping trip or a concert. Answer the questions in Exercise 1 for you. Make notes below.

4 Write about your special day. Use the notes you made in Exercise 3 and write about 50 words. Remember to use adjectives to make your writing more interesting.

VOCABULARY | Historical events

1 Find ten verbs in the past simple.

p	u	b	l	i	s	h	e	d
l	c	l	i	m	b	e	d	i
a	b	d	f	i	l	p	r	e
y	r	e	c	o	r	d	e	d
e	i	k	h	m	r	u	c	o
d	g	c	r	o	s	s	e	d
p	a	i	n	t	e	d	i	h
d	j	m	f	j	b	t	v	k
t	r	a	v	e	l	l	e	d
g	l	o	p	e	n	e	d	o

2 Choose the correct verbs to complete the sentences.

AMAZING WOMEN!

1 Emma Morano, from Italy, *died / recorded* in 2017. She was 117 years old.

2 Ariana Richards *painted / recorded* a picture called *Lady of the Dahlias* in 2009.

3 Malala Yousafzai *recorded / received* the Nobel Peace Prize when she was 17.

4 American Cassie De Pecol *travelled / crossed* to every country in the world.

5 Garbiñe Muguruza *opened / played* her first professional tennis match in 2012.

3 Complete the text with the verbs in the box.

> climbed   crossed   opened
> painted   published   travelled

Mrs Harlow lives next door to me. She has a quiet life now, but when she was young, her life was very interesting. She ¹_____ to many different places and had a lot of awesome experiences. She ²_____ Everest and she ³_____ the Atlantic Ocean in a boat. On her travels, she ⁴_____ a lot of beautiful pictures. When she returned to England, she ⁵_____ a shop and sold her pictures. She also ⁶_____ a book about her experiences. She's an amazing woman!

GRAMMAR Dates with *in* and *on*

1 Complete the table with the words and phrases in the box.

| 10th March | 2017 | August | October 2012 |
| Sunday | the 20th century | 12th June 1999 | |

in	on

2 Complete the sentences with *in* or *on*.

1 Lionel Messi played his first match for Barcelona _____ 16th October 2004.
2 Taylor Swift recorded her first album _____ 2006.
3 The British Museum in London opened _____ 15th January 1759.
4 Da Vinci painted the *Mona Lisa* _____ the 16th century.
5 Gareth Bale joined Real Madrid _____ 2013.

Past simple: regular verbs

3 Write the past simple form of the verbs.

1 complete _____
2 cook _____
3 copy _____
4 enjoy _____
5 finish _____
6 invite _____
7 join _____
8 phone _____
9 play _____
10 study _____

4 Rewrite the sentences in the past simple.

0 I help my parents at home.
I helped my parents at home.
1 I practise the guitar.
_____
2 I clean the bathroom.
_____
3 I play badminton with my friends.
_____
4 I phone my brother.
_____
5 I study maths, English and history.
_____

5 Correct the mistakes in the sentences.

1 Yesterday I go to school at 8 o'clock.
_____
2 I recieved an email from my teacher.
_____
3 Last weekend, I play football in the park.
_____
4 My brother watches TV yesterday.
_____
5 In the afternoon, it starts to rain and we went home.
_____

VOCABULARY Buildings

1 Match the words in the box to the photos.

| castle | cathedral | church | palace | square |

1 _____

2 _____

4 _____

3 _____

5 _____

2 Read the definitions and complete the words.

1 This covers the top of a house.
r __ __ __
2 You walk on this part of a room.
f __ __ __ __
3 You climb up these to get from one part of a house to another.
s __ __ __ __ __
4 The top part of a room.
c __ __ __ __ __ __
5 A person or animal made of stone.
s __ __ __ __ __

3 Complete the sentences with words from Exercises 1 and 2.

1 The _____ in our house is made of wood so it makes noise when you walk on it.
2 There is a big _____ of the king in front of the palace.
3 A _____ is a big, strong building, built in the past by important people. It protected the people inside.
4 The wind blew the _____ off the building.
5 The _____ is in the centre of town. It's flat and there are no houses so it's perfect for festivals.
6 She looked up at the paintings on the _____ of the church.

1 Look at the photos. What do you think happened? Choose words from the box. Then read the article and check your answers.

a fire	rain	a storm	an earthquake*

....

2 Read the article again. Are the sentences right (✓) or wrong (✗)?

1 The San Francisco fire happened in winter. ....
2 When the earthquake happened, a lot of people were at home. ....
3 The earthquake wasn't big. ....
4 The fires burned quickly. ....
5 People saved many buildings in the city. ....
6 28,000 people died. ....
7 People built the city again after the fire. ....

The Great Fire of
San Francisco

On 18th April 1906, there was an earthquake in the city of San Francisco. It was 5 o'clock in the morning and there weren't many people in the streets; most people were in bed. But it was a very big earthquake and people felt it in Los Angeles, more than 600 km from San Francisco. It destroyed many buildings.

But soon there was another problem. Many small fires started after the earthquake. At that time in San Francisco, the city was crowded and most old houses were made of wood. The fires moved quickly from building to building and from street to street. People didn't have water to stop the fire, and soon buildings all over the city were on fire.

The city burned for four days and it destroyed 28,000 buildings in the city. Around 250,000 people lost their homes and about 3,000 people died. After the fire, the people built a new city, with big streets and new houses.

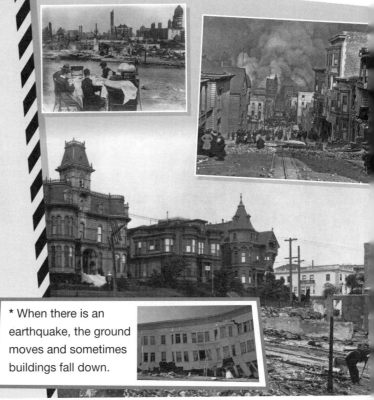

* When there is an earthquake, the ground moves and sometimes buildings fall down.

LISTENING

🔊 05 **1** Listen to the TV programme, *Our History*, and match the audience members to the people they ask about.

1 Robert .... **a** Valentina Tereshkova
2 Lisa .... **b** Henry VIII
3 Rachel .... **c** Marie Curie
4 Leon .... **d** Pelé

🔊 05 **2** Listen again. Tick (✓) the facts you hear.

1 King Henry VIII of England died in 1547. ....
2 Henry VIII had six wives. ....
3 The footballer Pelé played for Santos 638 times. ....
4 Pelé played international football for Brazil 92 times. ....
5 Marie Curie won the Nobel Prize in 1903. ....
6 Marie Curie died in 1934. ....
7 Valentina Tereshkova went to space in 1963. ....
8 Valentina Tereshkova's husband was also an astronaut. ....

1 Read the text and write the dates connected to the history of the camera on the timeline below.

Many years ago, people made pictures on a wall by letting the sun into a dark room through a tiny hole – they called this room a camera obscura. Before 1825 there were no photographs, but in 1829 Louis Daguerre invented the first camera. Then, in 1888, George Eastman invented the Kodak camera. After that, Steven Sasson invented the first digital camera in 1975. Now most people have a camera on their smartphone. We can all take photos.

0 Before
1825
no one took photos

1 _____
Louis Daguerre – first camera

2 _____
George Eastman – Kodak camera

3 _____
Steven Sasson – digital camera

4 _____
most people have a camera

2 Complete the sentences with the past simple form of the verbs in brackets.

1 Alexander Bell _____ (invent) the telephone.
2 People _____ (connect) to the internet.
3 People _____ (order) clothes, food and games online.
4 People _____ (start) to use mobile phones.
5 Children _____ (enjoy) computer games.
6 People _____ (save) time by using the internet.

3 Look at the information on the timeline. Then write about the invention of the internet. Use the verbs in brackets to help you. Write about 50 words.

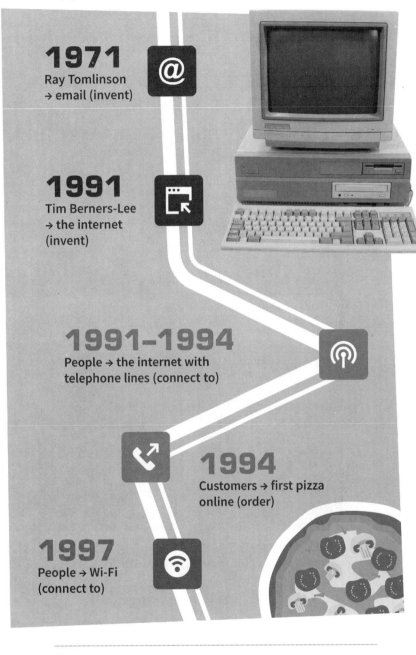

1971
Ray Tomlinson
→ email (invent)

1991
Tim Berners-Lee
→ the internet (invent)

1991–1994
People → the internet with telephone lines (connect to)

1994
Customers → first pizza online (order)

1997
People → Wi-Fi (connect to)

6 WHAT A GREAT JOB!

1 Choose the correct words to complete the sentences.

1 She's a *farmer / mechanic*.

2 He's a *cook / engineer*.

3 He's a *police officer / dentist*.

4 She's *an artist / a sports coach*.

5 He's *a manager / an actor*.

6 She's a *factory worker / shop assistant*.

7 He's a *photographer / model*.

8 She's a *pilot / nurse*.

2 Which job doesn't belong in each category?

In this job you need to …				
0 be artistic	actor	artist	(dentist)	photographer
1 wear a uniform	artist	police officer	nurse	dentist
2 work with people	nurse	police officer	dentist	farmer
3 work with machines	mechanic	actor	engineer	pilot
4 work outside	farmer	sports coach	factory worker	police officer

3 Complete the sentences with words in Exercise 1.

1 My brother is a _____. He works in a restaurant.
2 She repairs cars. She's a very good _____.
3 My sister is a _____. She teaches children football.
4 Photographers take his picture every day and he wears great clothes. He's a _____.
5 My dad works in a clothes shop. He's a _____.
6 My mum works on roads and buildings. She's an _____.

GRAMMAR — Past simple: negatives and questions

1 Complete the sentences with the past simple negative form of the verbs in brackets.

1 I _____ (do) my homework yesterday evening.
2 My mum _____ (study) English at school.
3 My father _____ (like) his job.
4 My parents _____ (go) to work last week. It was a holiday.
5 We _____ (meet) our friends at the party.
6 I _____ (walk) to school. I took the bus.

2 Put the words in the correct order to make questions.

1 time / did / open / the / what / shop / ?

2 did / to / yesterday / you / work / go / ?

3 parents / your / a factory / in / did / work / ?

4 the / come / did / office / she / to / ?

5 did / yesterday / what / do / you / ?

6 he / did / job / his / enjoy / ?

3 Match the questions in Exercise 2 to the answers below.

a Yes, she did. _____
b I went to school. _____
c At 10 o'clock. _____
d No, he didn't. _____
e Yes, they did. _____
f Yes, I did. _____

4 Correct the mistakes in the sentences.

👁 1 I don't go to school yesterday.

2 Did you watched the film on TV yesterday?

3 It was rainy and we don't play football.

4 Did you got a nice present for your birthday?

5 She didn't had English homework yesterday.

VOCABULARY — Work

1 Choose the correct words to complete the sentences.

1 My *boss / staff* is really nice. She gives me a lot of responsibility.
2 I would like to *start / earn* a lot of money.
3 My father works in a very big *customer / office* in the centre of the town.
4 We were very *busy / friendly* at work yesterday. There was no time for lunch.
5 I work in a shop. I help the *company / customers* with their shopping.
6 The *staff / business* all wear green shirts.

2 Complete the sentences with the words in Exercise 1.

1 There are ten people in my mother's _____. It's very big, with lots of desks and computers.
2 He was tired because he was very _____ at work.
3 The _____ at the supermarket work on Saturday mornings.
4 I served food to a lot of _____ in the restaurant.
5 Does your _____ give you a holiday in the summer?
6 Does your brother _____ money when he cleans cars?

1 Read the article. Which work experience would you prefer to do?

_____

2 For each question, choose the correct answer.

1 What kind of work did Dylan do with the photographer?
A studying families
B taking the bus
C helping the boss

2 What does Dylan say about his week?
A He didn't do many different things.
B He walked a long way.
C He enjoyed the work.

3 Why was Jake upset?
A He wanted to work in a different place.
B He didn't like the factory.
C He didn't like the staff at the factory.

4 What does Jake say about his week?
A It was long.
B It was good.
C It was boring.

5 What did Jake decide at the end of the week?
A He wants to work at the factory.
B He wants to leave school.
C He wants an interesting job.

WORK EXPERIENCE
Dylan and Jake did a week of work experience last month. How was it? Read on!

Dylan

I want to be a photographer and I worked in a photography studio. The photographer worked a lot with families and babies. It was great fun. I took the bus to her studio in a town near my home. On the first two days, we got things ready in the studio. On the last three days, we took photographs of some babies and their parents. I helped with everything! Every day was different and I learned a lot about the business.

Jake

I worked in a factory. My plan isn't to be a factory worker – I want to be an engineer. At first I was upset. I thought factory work was boring, but it wasn't boring at all. The factory makes special seats for planes and we tested them. It was very interesting! The factory opened at 7 am and closed at 5 pm. It was a long day! Often I was very busy and I didn't have much time for lunch! But I really enjoyed the work. I want to work there when I leave school.

LISTENING

🔊 06 **1** Listen to the conversation between Lauren and Ben about work experience. Choose the correct person.

1 *Lauren / Ben* went to work by train.
2 *Lauren / Ben* worked in an office.
3 *Lauren / Ben* started at 8 o'clock in the morning.
4 *Lauren / Ben* liked the staff.
5 *Lauren / Ben* didn't wear a T-shirt.

🔊 06 **2** Listen again and answer the questions.

1 Where did Lauren want to do her work experience?

2 Why did Lauren use her bike to go to work?

3 Why was Ben's job interesting?

4 What time did Ben start work?

5 What did Ben wear to work?

6 Who did Lauren work with?

WRITING — A paragraph about work

1 Read the text and answer the questions.

1 Where did the writer's dad work?

2 Did he enjoy his job?

2 Read the text again and add the punctuation below.

a three capital letters
b three full stops
c two apostrophes

3 You are going to write about a job that John did. Look at the questions and match them to John's answers.

1 Where did you work?
2 What time did you start and finish?
3 Did you earn a lot of money?
4 What did you wear?
5 Did you enjoy your job?

a yes, it was hard work but fun – the people were friendly
b in a fish factory
c blue trousers and a blue jacket
d no
e 6 o'clock and 2 o'clock

4 Write a paragraph about John's job. Use the information in Exercise 3 and write about 50 words. Remember to use capital letters, full stops and apostrophes correctly.

My dad's first job

My dad worked in an office in a school. he started work at 8 o'clock and he finished at 3 o'clock He didnt earn much money, but the people were very friendly and he liked the students my dad used a computer at work for the first time in 1981 my dads job was fun because it was busy.

7 AN EXCITING TRIP

VOCABULARY Holidays

1 Match the verbs to the nouns to make holiday activities.

0	go	c	**a**	on the beach
1	buy		**b**	camping
2	go		**c**	sightseeing
3	do		**d**	at a hotel
4	ride		**e**	photos
5	stay		**f**	presents
6	lie		**g**	water sports
7	take		**h**	a bike

1 ....   2 ....

2 Match the phrases in Exercise 1 to the photos.

3 ....   4 ....

5 ....   6 ....   7 ....   8 ....

3 Complete the sentences with the holiday activities in Exercise 1.

1 We always .... on holiday. Last year, our room was very big!
2 This year, I can .... with my new camera.
3 I want to ...., like sailing, windsurfing and surfing.
4 Do you want to .... in the shop? You can get something for your mum.
5 We sometimes .... all day. It's hot, but the sea is cold.
6 I want to .... in London. There are lots of famous buildings.
7 I sometimes .... when we go on holiday. It's a great way to travel around and see places!
8 Let's .... this summer! I love sleeping in a tent when it isn't cold at night.

GRAMMAR Past simple: irregular verbs

1 Find 12 irregular verbs in the wordsnake.

ridehavegivetakegoseebuygetupcomeswimdoeat

1	4	7	10 ....
2	5	8	11 ....
3	6	9	12 ....

2 Write the past simple form of the verbs in Exercise 1.

1	4	7	10 ....
2	5	8	11 ....
3	6	9	12 ....

3 Complete the text with verbs in Exercise 2.

Last summer, I ¹ _____ on holiday to Paris with my parents and sister. My sister's friend ² _____ with us, too. We ³ _____ an amazing time. We ⁴ _____ very nice food. Mum ⁵ _____ lots of photos. We ⁶ _____ interesting buildings and famous museums and we ⁷ _____ bikes around the city. My parents ⁸ _____ me some money and I ⁹ _____ some postcards and a T-shirt.

4 Write questions in the past simple. Then match the questions to the answers below.

1 Where / you / go on holiday / last year?
_____

2 Who / you / go with?
_____

3 your sister / go sightseeing / with you?
_____

4 What food / you / eat?
_____

5 you and your family / enjoy / the holiday?
_____

a I went with my family.
b We ate fish and a lot of ice cream.
c Yes, we did.
d I went to Majorca.
e No, she didn't.

5 Correct the mistakes in the sentences.

👁 1 I go to France last summer.
_____

2 I was sightseeing when I was in New York.
_____

3 I bough some postcards and a T-shirt.
_____

4 My parents give me some money for my birthday last year.
_____

5 Did you ate some nice food in Italy?
_____

VOCABULARY   Holidays

1 Complete the holiday words with the missing vowels.

0 a _i_ r p _o_ r t
1 c _ _ _ c h
2 f _ _ r r y
3 f l _ _ g h t

4 g _ _ _ d _ _ b _ _ _ k
5 m _ p
6 p _ _ s s p _ _ r t
7 s t _ _ t _ _ _ n

8 s _ _ _ t c _ _ s _
9 t _ c k _ t
10 t _ _ _ r _ s t
11 t _ _ _ r g _ _ _ d _

2 Choose the correct verbs to complete the sentences.

1 We *arrived at / got off* the hotel at 10 o'clock at night.
2 Did you *pack / catch* the guidebook in your suitcase?
3 When we *got on / arrived* the bus, there weren't any seats.
4 The journey *got off / took* 12 hours!
5 Did you *arrive at / travel by* ferry to France or did you fly?
6 We *got off / packed* the train when we arrived at our station.
7 Can I *travel by / catch* a bus to Manchester from here?

1 Read the article about two famous travellers and complete the table.

What was his name?	1 	Ferdinand Magellan
Where was he born?	Morocco	4
When was he born?	2	5
Where did he go?	3	6

TRAVELLING THE WORLD

Today, many people travel around the world. It isn't difficult or expensive. We know a lot about places that are far away. But in the past, it was very different. Read on to find out about two famous travellers from history.

Ibn Battuta was born in Morocco in 1304. When he was a young man, Battuta studied and never travelled far from his home in Morocco. But, when he was 21 years old, he left home and travelled for almost 30 years. He went to 44 countries, including India and China. He visited famous cities, such as Granada, Beijing and Cairo. Battuta wrote about his travels when he was an old man.

Ferdinand Magellan was born in Portugal in 1480. His parents were rich, but they died when Magellan was young. In 1505, he became a sailor and travelled to Africa and India. In 1519, he left Spain with five ships and crossed the Atlantic Ocean. The journey was very dangerous and they arrived in the Philippines about 18 months later. Only one ship returned to Spain. Magellan didn't have GPS and only used maps and the stars to find his way. He is famous for being the first man from Europe to cross the Pacific Ocean.

2 Read the article again and answer the questions. Write complete sentences.

1 What did Ibn Battuta do before he left home?

2 How many years did Ibn Battuta travel for?

3 How many countries did Ibn Battuta go to?

4 What did he do when he was an old man?

5 When did Magellan become a sailor?

6 How long did the journey from Spain to the Philippines take?

7 How did Magellan find his way?

LISTENING

🔊 07 **1** Listen to the conversation between two friends. What does Paul give Rebecca?

....

🔊 07 **2** Listen again. Who says what? Write 'P' (Paul) or 'R' (Rebecca).

1 How was your holiday? ....
2 I went to Spain too! ....
3 We were there at the same time! ....
4 Who did you go with? ....
5 Where did you stay? ....
6 Did you try Spanish food? ....

🔊 07 **3** Listen again and match the questions to the answers.

1 How long did Paul stay in Spain? ....
2 How long did Rebecca stay in Spain? ....
3 Who did Paul go to Spain with? ....
4 Who did Rebecca go to Spain with? ....
5 Where did Paul stay? ....
6 Where did Rebecca stay? ....

a mum and brother
b two weeks
c on a campsite
d mum and dad
e in a hotel
f a week

WRITING A description of a holiday

1 Read the text. Tick (✓) the questions Marta answers.

1 Where did you go? ....
2 Who did you go with? ....
3 How did you travel? ....
4 Where did you stay? ....
5 What did you do? ....
6 What did you eat? ....
7 What did you buy? ....

My holiday ☀
– Marta

Last year I went to Granada with my parents. We flew there. It took three hours. We stayed in a hotel in the city centre. We went sightseeing and visited the Alhambra. It's beautiful! We ate some excellent fish and I tried gazpacho. It's a Spanish soup. I liked Granada a lot. We had a really good time.

2 Think about a holiday you had. Answer the questions in Exercise 1 for you. Make notes below.

....
....
....
....

3 Write about your holiday. Use your notes in Exercise 2 and write about 50 words.

....
....
....
....
....
....

8 FAVOURITE PLACES

Bedroom furniture

1 Match the words in the box to the photos.

armchair	blanket	bookshelf	carpet	chest of drawers
cupboard	curtains	cushions	lamp	mirror	photographs

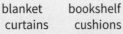

1 _____

2 _____

3 _____

4 _____

5 _____

6 _____

7 _____

8 _____

9 _____

10 _____

11 _____

2 Read the clues and write the words.

1 You can see your face in this. _____
2 You put things like books or clothes on or inside these three objects. _____
3 This covers the floor. _____
4 You use this when it is dark at night. _____
5 This is warm and you put it on your bed. _____

3 Complete the text with the correct form of words in Exercise 1.

My bedroom is big and I love it. It's got two windows with long ¹_____ and a big ²_____ where I can sit. But I sometimes sit on the floor on the ³_____. There are some big ⁴_____ on the floor, too. They are very comfortable to sit on. There's a big ⁵_____ with books and my computer games, and a ⁶_____ of my friends on the wall.

1 Complete the table with the correct words.

	every	some	any	no
A place	everywhere	3	5	7
A thing	1	4	anything	nothing
A person	2	someone	6	no one

2 Choose the correct words to complete the sentences.

1 *Anyone / No one* could answer the question. It was very difficult.
2 There wasn't *anything / anywhere* in the cupboard.
3 I had *nothing / anything* to do yesterday.
4 I want to go *someone / somewhere* interesting for my holidays.
5 Did *anyone / anywhere* pass the maths exam?
6 We saw interesting shops *everywhere / everything* in the city.

3 Match the sentence halves.

1 Did Mark have _____
2 There's nothing _____
3 Is there anywhere _____
4 I want to go _____
5 Can I have _____
6 No one told me _____
7 Did anyone _____
8 Someone _____

a something to drink, please?
b you liked tennis.
c anything to say about the accident?
d see that great film on TV last night?
e on TV tonight.
f we can go on Saturday?
g gave me a present for my birthday.
h somewhere quiet to read.

4 Correct the mistakes in the sentences.

1 Some one gave me a T-shirt.

2 He didn't bring nothing to the party.

3 We stayed at home all day and we didn't go everywhere.

4 You didn't tell me any thing about it!

5 Please bring somthing to eat to the party.

1 Complete the verbs with the missing letters.

1 d_____ pictures
2 p_____ computer games, the drums, the guitar, music, songs
3 w_____ stories, a diary, a song
4 l_____ t_____ music, the sound of the sea, stories
5 r_____ a diary, a magazine
6 p_____ pictures

2 Complete the text with the words in the box.

computer	drums	pictures	songs	stories	wind

My special place

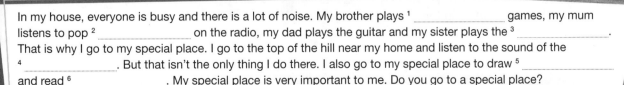

In my house, everyone is busy and there is a lot of noise. My brother plays ¹ _____ games, my mum listens to pop ² _____ on the radio, my dad plays the guitar and my sister plays the ³ _____ . That is why I go to my special place. I go to the top of the hill near my home and listen to the sound of the ⁴ _____ . But that isn't the only thing I do there. I also go to my special place to draw ⁵ _____ and read ⁶ _____ . My special place is very important to me. Do you go to a special place?

1 Read the notices and messages and <u>underline</u> the bedroom furniture words.

2 For each question, choose the correct answer.

1

Mexican blankets
Different sizes
Buy one for £20 or two for £35

Today only!

A The blankets are all big.
B There's a special offer on these blankets.
C The blankets are only £35 each today.

2

Wanted

Chest of drawers, 100–120 cm tall.
Can pay up to £50.
Phone Beth after 5 pm.
01632 960321

A Beth wants to sell her chest of drawers.
B Beth wants people to phone her in the evening.
C The chest of drawers Beth wants can be any size.

3

Hi Dan,
Your bedroom is amazing! Mine's big, but it's so boring. How can I make it special? Can you give me some ideas?
Luke

Why did Luke write this message to Dan?
A He wants some help to change his room.
B He wants to see his friend, Dan.
C He wants a bigger room.

4

Grey armchair with cushions
Old but comfortable
£20
Ask inside for more information

A The armchair is uncomfortable.
B The armchair has cushions.
C The cushions are £20.

5

Anna,
Are you busy this afternoon? Let's go to the park. I haven't got any homework and I can be there at 5 pm. Answer me before 4.30 pm.
Carla

A Carla needs Anna's help with some homework.
B Carla wants to see Anna in the park later today.
C Carla can't go to the park because she is at school until 5 pm.

6

Art competition

Draw a building in the town
and win an art book.
Open to students in Year 7.

A You can draw anything you like for the competition.
B Everyone can enter the competition.
C There is a prize for the winner of the competition.

LISTENING

🔊 **08** **1** Listen to the interview with a teenage blogger about her favourite place at home. Is KJ's favourite room big or small?

....

🔊 **08** **2** Listen again and choose the correct answers.

1 People .... read KJ Neal's blog.
   A in Wales   **B** all over the world
2 KJ is .... years old.
   A 14   **B** 13
3 Her .... is her favourite place.
   A writing room   **B** bedroom
4 KJ's favourite thing is her ....
   A lamp   **B** armchair

🔊 **08** **3** Listen again. Are the sentences right (✓) or wrong (✗)?

1 KJ's birthday is in January. ....
2 She's from Scotland. ....
3 She doesn't like her bedroom. ....
4 She doesn't share the writing room with anyone. ....
5 There are some curtains in the writing room. ....
6 She sometimes writes in her bedroom. ....

WRITING   A description of your favourite thing

1 Read the text. Number the questions in the order Matthew answers them.

a What does it look like? ....
b Where is it from? ....
c Why do you like it? ....
d Where is it now? ....
e What is your favourite thing? ....

My favourite thing
by Matthew

My favourite thing is an old photograph. My dad gave it to me when I was little so it's special. It shows my mum and dad when they were young. In the photo, they are on the beach and they are laughing. The photo is on a bookshelf in my bedroom. I like it because they look very happy.

2 Look at the text again and find one sentence with *because* and one sentence with *so*. Then choose the correct words to complete the rules.

1 We use *because* / *so* to say why we do something.
2 We use *because* / *so* to show the result of something

3 Complete the sentences with *because* or *so*.

1 I like my bedroom .... it's small.
2 Our house is small .... I share a room with my sister.
3 I like animals .... I have some magazines about dogs, cats and wild animals.
4 I like computer games .... they are fun.

4 Think about your favourite thing. Answer the questions in Exercise 1 for you. Make notes below.

....
....
....
....

5 Write about your favourite thing. Use the notes you made in Exercise 4 and write about 50 words. Remember to use *because* and *so* in your text.

....
....
....
....
....
....
....
....
....
....

VOCABULARY Clothes

1 Match the words in the box to the photos.

> boots   cap   gloves   jumper   scarf   socks   suit   sunglasses
> swimming costume   swimming shorts   tie   trainers

1 _____

2 _____

3 _____

4 _____

5 _____

6 _____

7 _____

8 _____

9 _____

10 _____

11 _____

12 _____

2 Where do you wear the clothes? Complete the table with the words in Exercise 1. Some words can go in more than one column.

at the beach	on your feet	on your head	when it's cold	at work in an office

3 Choose the correct words to complete the sentences.

1 My favourite jumper is *right / bright* red.
2 I like your new *black / sun* boots.
3 My dad wears a *pale / bright* grey suit to work.
4 My swimming costume is purple and *pale / blue*.

1 Match the sentences.

1 It's my pen. _____
2 It's your phone. _____
3 They're his books. _____
4 They're our jumpers. _____
5 They're her pencils. _____
6 They're their bags. _____

a It's yours.
b They're hers.
c They're theirs.
d It's mine.
e They're his.
f They're ours.

2 Look at the words in brackets and complete the sentences with the correct determiners.

0 This is my jumper and that's _____*his*_____ (Cameron's jumper).
1 This isn't Clara's cap. I think that cap is _____ (Clara's cap).
2 I've got your mobile, but I can't find _____ (my mobile).
3 This is my bag. Where's _____ (your bag)?
4 That is your computer and this is _____ (our computer).
5 These are our trainers and those are _____ (Daniel and Lucia's trainers).

3 Correct the mistakes in the sentences.

1 She watches TV in free time.
_____

2 Can I borrow you new sunglasses?
_____

3 It's a birthday on Sunday. I'm having a party.
_____

4 My mum bought my some new trainers for school.
_____
_____

5 This jacket isn't your. It's mine.
_____

4 Choose the correct words.

1 Harry loves *his / her / its* dog and takes it for a walk every day.
2 Can you help me with *your / my / their* homework?
3 I've got *your / yours / ours* tickets for the concert.
4 This book isn't *my / mine / me*.
5 The students are writing stories in *they / theirs / their* English class today.
6 Sarah left *hers / her / his* coat in the playground.

1 Complete the words with the missing vowels.

1 w __ __ l
2 c __ t t __ n
3 l __ __ t h __ r
4 p l __ s t __ c
5 m __ t __ l
6 c __ r k

2 Complete the sentences with the words in the box.

cotton	leather	plastic	metal	wool

1 My shirt is made of _____.
2 Mobile phones and tablets are usually made of _____.
3 My winter jumper is warm because it's made of _____.
4 Water bottles are usually made of _____.
5 My boots were expensive because they're made of _____.

1 Look at the photos and the title. What do you think the article is about? Choose the best answer. Then read the article and check your ideas.

   A shopping for clothes
   B a fashion show
   C clothes and the environment

Fast fashion

Do you like fashion? Are you wearing new clothes? Do you buy new clothes every month? For many people, the answer to these questions is 'yes'. In the past, people didn't buy many clothes. They gave their old clothes to their brothers and sisters, or recycled them in the home. But today, many clothes are cheap. People buy clothes and they only wear them two or three times. They don't want them after two or three months. We call this 'fast fashion'. It's fun, but it's bad for the environment.

Everyone needs clothes, but how can you help the environment? Here are some ideas.

1. Don't buy many new things. Buy one good T-shirt, not six cheap ones.

2. Recycle your old clothes. We all have clothes at home that we don't wear. Some people sell their clothes online, or swap them with friends. You can give good clothes to a charity shop and send very old or damaged clothes to a recycling centre.

3. Buy recycled clothes and accessories. Matt and Nat is a company that makes bags. But the bags aren't made of leather – they're made of 100% recycled bottles! The company also uses cork and rubber for its bags.

You can love fashion and also love the environment!

2 Read the article again. Are the sentences right (✓) or wrong (✗)?

   1 In the past, people recycled their clothes.
   2 It's now possible to buy many clothes without spending a lot of money.
   3 'Fast fashion' is when you buy things quickly.
   4 You can sell your old clothes to a recycling centre.
   5 The bags at Matt and Nat are made of plastic.

3 Find words or phrases in the text to match the meanings.

   1 the air, water, land and animals around us
   2 give one thing and get another thing for it
   3 this shop sells things to get money to help people, places or animals
   4 people recycle things here
   5 when something is broken or not in perfect condition

LISTENING

🔊 **1** Listen to Julie talking to her dad. Why does she ask her dad for help?

....

🔊 **2** Listen again and write one word for each answer.

1 The School Family Day is next ....
2 The students want to sell things to help .... in poor countries.
3 Julie's dad says she can make necklaces with ....
4 Julie wants to give her .... dress and some ....
5 Julie should ask her .... for help to find clothes for the School Family Day.

WRITING   A text about your favourite clothes

1 Complete the texts with the words in the boxes.

cotton	made	parents	wear

My favourite clothes

I've got a blue dress and a red jacket. I bought them last year with some money my ¹ .... gave me for my birthday. I sometimes ² .... the dress at school in summer. It is made of ³ .... The jacket is very special. It is ⁴ .... of leather. I wear it when I meet my friends in town at the weekend.

green	leather	park	trainers

My favourite clothes

I love my new ⁵ .... My mum bought them for me last week. They are blue and white, and they are made of ⁶ .... I wear them in the afternoon when I go to the ⁷ .... I also like my ⁸ .... shorts. I often wear them on holiday on the beach.

Clara

Hugo

2 Read the texts again and complete the table.

	Favourite clothes	Colour	Material	When?	Where?
Clara	dress	¹	cotton	in ²	at ³ ....
	⁴	red	leather	at the ⁵	in town
Hugo	trainers	blue and ⁶	leather	in the afternoon	at the park
	⁷	green	----------	on holiday	on the ⁸ ....

3 Complete the table with information about your favourite clothes.

	Favourite clothes	Colours	Material	When?	Where?
You					

4 Write about your favourite clothes. Use the information in the table in Exercise 3 and write about 50 words.

....

....

....

....

10 BUYING THINGS

VOCABULARY Buying and selling

1 Find eight shopping words.

o	b	p	r	i	c	e	c
d	n	t	e	r	d	p	w
i	c	d	c	h	e	t	a
s	a	l	e	s	m	g	l
c	s	f	i	b	i	l	l
o	h	w	p	u	r	s	e
u	p	g	t	i	w	s	t
n	c	s	o	b	n	r	u
t	l	l	k	i	c	f	e

2 Choose the correct words to complete the text.

What kind of shopper am I? Well, I'm careful because I haven't got a lot of money. There's never any [1] *cash / bills* in my wallet! I always look at the [2] *bill / price* before I buy something. I don't spend a lot of money on clothes. I usually look for things with a [3] *discount / cash*. Last week, I got a great new T-shirt. It was only £3 in the [4] *discount / sale*. I always keep the [5] *bill / receipt* when I buy something.

3 Complete the sentences with words from Exercise 1. Sometimes more than one answer is possible.

1 My sister got some trainers in a _____. They were half price!
2 Tom lost his _____ in the shop. He had £20 in it.
3 I bought my mum a new leather _____ for her birthday.
4 I lost the _____ for my new jumper so I couldn't take it back.
5 My dad paid the _____ because I didn't have enough money.
6 How much are these sunglasses? I can't see the _____.

1 Complete the rules with the phrases in the box.

> countable   countable and uncountable
> negative   positive   uncountable

1 We use *some* in _____ sentences with countable nouns.
2 We use *any* in _____ sentences with uncountable nouns.
3 We use *a lot of* with _____ nouns.
4 We use *a few* with _____ nouns.
5 We use *a bit of* with _____ nouns.

2 Put the words in the correct order to make sentences and questions.

1 there / a / people / café / the / lot / were / of / in

2 for / my / birthday / books / some / I / would / like

3 any / have / you / do / money / ?

4 boots / any / football / got / brother / hasn't / my

5 few / a / biscuits / my / buy / to / sister / wants

6 cake / bit / of / a / you / like / would / ?

3 Choose the correct words or phrases to complete the sentences.

1 My sister has got *a lot of* / *any* friends.
2 We've got *a few* / *a bit of* packets of crisps in our cupboard.
3 My friends haven't got *some* / *any* pets.
4 Do you have *a bit of* / *a few* time to go shopping with me?
5 My brother bought *any* / *some* new shoes.
6 I've got *a lot of* / *a few* books. I counted them yesterday. I've got 54!

4 Correct the mistakes in the sentences.

1 I've got a bread and an apple.

2 There aren't some cookies in the kitchen.

3 There are a many new students in my class.

4 I've got lot of books in my bag.

5 These trainers cost much money.

1 Match the sentence halves.

1 I sold my T-shirt to Luke _____
2 What's English _____
3 Did you buy food _____
4 My parents paid _____
5 Canada is famous _____
6 Did you have a party _____

a for the tickets.
b for your birthday?
c for £5.
d for the party on Saturday?
e for *patatas*?
f for its mountains and cold winters.

2 Complete the sentences with the verbs in the box and *for*.

> buy   have   is   pay   sell

1 I can't _____ the tickets today because I haven't got enough money.
2 I want to _____ my sister some flowers _____ her birthday.
3 Kyle is going to _____ his old T-shirts _____ £2 each.
4 We are going to _____ a party _____ the end of exams.
5 Rio de Janeiro in Brazil _____ famous _____ its beaches.

1 **Read about two of the biggest shopping centres in the world. Which one do you think is the most interesting?**

West Edmonton Mall

West Edmonton Mall is a shopping centre in Canada. It's really big! You can spend your holidays in this shopping centre because there are hotels, cinemas, a water park, and lots and lots of shops. Teenagers like to spend the day in Galaxyland. This is the largest indoor amusement park in the world. There are 24 rides and places to play. You can play mini-golf or go ice skating. You can swim and go down 21 slides in the water park. The weather is not important because everything is inside. Do you like films? There are 13 different films at the cinema every evening. Come to see this shopping centre. It's open 365 days a year.

Dubai Mall

The Dubai Mall is in the United Arab Emirates. It opened in 2008 and now has more than 1,200 shops. There are 200 restaurants as well. Families can spend time in the shopping centre because there are a lot of activities for young people. One of the best places to go is the aquarium. You can stand in a tunnel under the water and see the fish swimming above you, or you can ride in a boat with a glass bottom and see the fish underneath you. Another great place for teenagers is Kidzania. This is a little city where you can try different jobs. You can be a dentist, a police officer or work in a restaurant or a supermarket. You sell and pay for things with special money. It's a great place!

2 **Read the texts again and answer the questions.**

WEST EDMONTON MALL
1 Where is West Edmonton Mall? ....
2 Can you sleep there? ....
3 What is Galaxyland? ....
4 Can you swim in the water park when it is raining? ....

DUBAI MALL
5 When did Dubai Mall open? ....
6 How many restaurants are there? ....
7 What can you see in the boat in the aquarium? ....
8 What jobs can you try in Kidzania? ....

LISTENING

🔊 10

1 Listen to five short conversations. For each question, choose the correct answer.

1 You will hear Katie talking about a present for her mother. What did she buy?
 A something to wear
 B something to read
 C something to eat

2 You will hear two friends talking during their lunch break. What do they decide to do together after school?
 A go to the girl's house
 B go to the swimming pool
 C go to the library

3 You will hear a man talking to his daughter. What does his daughter want to buy?
 A some shoes
 B a dress
 C a jacket

4 You will hear a teenager talking to his mother. What does he want to do?
 A He wants to ride his bike.
 B He wants to sell his bike.
 C He wants to take his bike on holiday.

5 You will hear a boy talking to a shop assistant. Why does he buy the yellow T-shirt?
 A because it's cheap
 B because it's big
 C because he likes the colour

WRITING A story

1 Read the text about a day out in a shopping centre. What did the family buy?

....

> Last Sunday I went to a shopping centre near my house. I went with my mother, my father and my sister. We arrived at 10 o'clock. First, I went with my sister and my parents to look at clothes. It was my sister's birthday and we bought her a new jacket. It only cost £15 because there was a sale. For lunch we went to an Italian restaurant and ate pizza. After that, my parents wanted to go to the supermarket, but my sister and I didn't, so we went to the music shop. There were a few good albums but we didn't buy any. Then, we all went to the cinema to see a film. Finally, at 7 o'clock we went home for dinner. It was a great day out!

2 You are going to write a story about a day out at a shopping centre. It can be a true story or you can invent it. Think about answers to these questions. Make notes.

1 Where is the shopping centre?

2 When did you go?

3 Who did you go with?

4 What did you do first?

5 Did you buy anything?

6 Did you do anything else?

7 Did you enjoy the day?

3 Write your story about a day out at a shopping centre. Use the notes you made in Exercise 2 and write about 50 words. Remember to use the words *after that*, *after*, *later* and *finally* to link the events in your story.

VOCABULARY Food

1 Which word doesn't belong in each group?

0	(mushrooms) fruit juice	mineral water lemonade
1	burger chicken legs	ice cream pizza
2	vegetables salad	mushrooms cola
3	cheesecake fruit salad	burger ice cream
4	chips rice	vegetables chicken legs
5	pasta vanilla	strawberry chocolate

2 Choose the correct words to complete the sentences.

1 I'd like a *bowl* / *glass* of fruit juice.
2 Can I have a slice of *pizza* / *water*?
3 Do you want a *bottle* / *piece* of cake?
4 I've got a bottle of *lemonade* / *rice* for the picnic.
5 I ate a *bowl* / *slice* of pasta for lunch.
6 Would you like a *glass* / *plate* of chips?

3 Complete the sentences with the words in the box.

chicken legs	salad	lemonade
cream	strawberries	tomato

1 _____ comes from cow's milk.
2 I like pasta with _____ sauce.
3 There are two _____ on the plate with the rice and salad.
4 The ingredients for my favourite _____ are tomatoes, lettuce, onions and cheese.
5 I love drinking _____ when I go to a restaurant.
6 My dad always buys _____. They are his favourite fruit.

GRAMMAR   Comparative adjectives; as … as

1 Complete the sentences with *as … as* or *not as … as* and the adjectives in brackets.

0 In winter, Russia is very cold. Colombia isn't cold. In winter, Colombia is *not as cold as* Russia. (cold)

1 Oliver is 12 years old and Jessie is 12 years old. Oliver is _____ Jessie. (old)

2 Jake is 1.50 m tall. Freddy is 1.45 m tall. Freddy is _____ Jake. (tall)

3 The apartment has got two bedrooms. The house has got four bedrooms. The apartment is _____ the house. (big)

4 The film is very interesting. The book is very good, too. The book is _____ the film. (interesting)

5 The basketball costs £15. The football costs £10. The football is _____ the basketball. (expensive)

6 My friends like Jenny. They all like Sarah, too. Sarah is _____ Jenny. (popular)

2 Write the comparative form of the adjectives.

1 long _____
2 healthy _____
3 short _____
4 exciting _____
5 hot _____
6 popular _____

3 Complete the sentences with the comparative adjectives in Exercise 2.

1 Football is a _____ sport than tennis in most countries.

2 It's _____ in summer in the south of Italy than in the south of England.

3 Trousers are _____ than shorts.

4 I'm _____ than my sister. She's very tall!

5 I love video games. They are _____ than watching boring TV.

6 Fruit and vegetables are _____ than sweets and cakes.

4 Complete the second sentence so that it means the same as the first sentence.

0 Pizza isn't as healthy as salad. Salad is *healthier* than pizza.

1 New York is bigger than San Francisco. San Francisco isn't _____ as New York.

2 My bike is cleaner than your bike. Your bike is _____ than my bike.

3 Cheesecake isn't as nice as chocolate cake. Chocolate cake is _____ than cheesecake.

4 The sun is hotter than the moon. The moon is _____ than the sun.

5 History is more boring than maths. History isn't as _____ maths.

5 Choose the correct words.

◉ 1 I went to the park with my *old / older* sister.
2 The English test was as *easy / easier* as the maths test.
3 My friend's house is *biggest / bigger* than mine.
4 My brother is *younger / more young* than me.
5 He plays the piano *better / well* than his sister.

VOCABULARY   Food

1 Put the letters in *italics* in the correct order to complete the sentences.

1 My mum often makes a wonderful soup with *deslono* _____ and my dad likes making *kanepsca* _____ for breakfast at the weekends.

2 I don't like *ililhc* _____ in my food. I tried *rucry* _____ but it was very hot!

3 In my country we make *telmosete* _____ with *pichs* _____, and sometimes with fried *inonso* _____.

4 My sister has terrible teeth because she eats a lot of *etwess* _____.

5 When we go on holiday to the beach, we sometimes eat *dofeoas* _____ or *lidregl emat* _____.

READING

1 Read the review and choose the best title.

  A A great meal
  B Restaurants in my town
  C American food

I had a wonderful day yesterday! It was my 14th birthday and my parents took me to the fantastic new American restaurant in our town. Do you know it? It's next to the cinema. I had a burger and chips for my main course and I drank an amazing glass of lemonade that was made with fresh lemons! My mum had an omelette and a salad, and my dad had chicken legs. The restaurant is very popular. It was so busy! We had to wait to get our food, but that was OK. Everyone was very friendly and there was a band playing music!

The best part of the meal was dessert. I had chocolate cake. My mum had fruit salad and cream, but Dad didn't have anything. At the end of the meal, the manager came over to our table. 'Happy birthday, young man,' he said. 'Would you like your present now?' Do you know what my present was? My meal! My parents didn't have to pay for it! We were all very surprised. It was a brilliant evening.

Danny

2 Read the review again. What did the family eat? Complete the table.

	Main course	Dessert
Danny	1	2
Danny's mum	3	4
Danny's dad	5	6

3 Read the review again and answer the questions.

  1 Why did Danny go to the restaurant?

  2 Where is the restaurant?

  3 Were there many people at the restaurant?

  4 Who said 'Happy birthday' to Danny?

  5 How much did Danny's parents pay for his meal?

LISTENING

🔊 **1** Listen to the conversation between two friends, Josh and Lily. What does Josh like eating?

....

🔊 **2** Listen again and choose the correct answers.

1 Lily goes to classes on *Wednesdays / Thursdays*.
2 The classes start at *4 pm / 5.30 pm*.
3 Lily pays *£15 / £20* a month for the classes.
4 There are *13 / 30* students in the class.
5 Last week Lily learned to make *curry / pizza*.
6 The teacher's phone number is *01632 960875 / 01632 960578*.
7 Lily goes to classes in *a restaurant / London*.

WRITING · A text about food at a festival

1 Complete the table with the words in the box.

~~American~~	brilliant	burger and chips	cheese pizza	chocolate cake	cola	~~fantastic~~
fruit salad	Italian	lemonade	lovely	Mexican	mineral water	omelette and salad
orange juice	pasta with meat	Spanish	strawberry cheesecake	vanilla ice cream	wonderful	

Type of food	Main courses	Desserts	Drinks	Opinions
American				*fantastic*

2 Complete the text about a street festival with the words in the box.

cola	dancing	hot	meat	summer

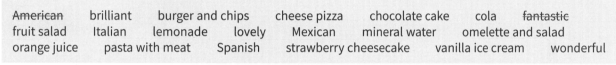

A *street* festival

My name's Mario and I live in Spain. Every
¹ .... we have a big festival in my
village. There is music, ² .... and
lots of street food. I go out with my friends
and family. The food I like best is potatoes,
especially with ³ .... and chilli.
They also sell ⁴ .... or other
soft drinks. We dance until really late. My
parents always buy me a cup of delicious
⁵ .... chocolate at midnight.
It's wonderful!

Mario (Spain)

3 Think about a special festival where you live and the food you can eat there. Answer the questions. Make notes.

1 When is the festival?
....

2 What can you do at the festival?
....

3 Who do you go to the festival with?
....

4 What can you eat and drink there?
....

4 Write about your festival. Use the notes you made in Exercise 3 and write about 50 words.

....
....
....
....
....
....

VOCABULARY Technology

1 Use the photos to complete the crossword.

Down

Across

2 Match the words in Exercise 1 to the definitions.

1 You use this to know how much exercise you do.

2 You wear these on your ears to listen to music.

3 You can carry this small computer around with you.

4 You click on this object with your finger when you work on a computer.

5 You can read books on this machine.

6 You use this machine to put images and text from your computer onto paper.

7 You need this machine to play video games.

8 This is a type of modern telephone.

9 This is a very small flat computer. You use your fingers to control it.

10 This part of a computer shows pictures or words.

11 This part of a computer has letters and numbers on it.

12 Sound comes out of this part of a computer.

3 Choose the correct words to complete the sentences.

1 I use *screens* / *headphones* to listen to music when I'm on the bus.

2 My father has *an e-reader* / *a console* where he keeps his books.

3 My parents gave me a new games *speaker* / *console* for my birthday.

4 Have you got a smartphone with a *printer* / *screen* you can touch?

5 The teacher told us to use the school *printer* / *tracker* for our pictures.

6 I'd like a *keyboard* / *laptop* so I can study in any room in the house.

1 Write the superlative form of the adjectives.

1 good
2 bad
3 fast
4 exciting
5 heavy
6 famous
7 clever
8 thin

2 Complete the sentences with superlative adjectives in Exercise 1.

1 The _____ man in the world weighed 675 kilos.
2 Jenny won first prize for the _____ story in the competition.
3 Kevin is the _____ student in the class. He's very intelligent.
4 Everybody knows Buckingham Palace. It is one of the _____ buildings in London.
5 The film was terrible. It is the _____ film this year.

3 Choose the correct words to complete the sentences.

1 Nicky is the *more friendly / friendliest* person in my class.
2 Rome is one of the *oldest / older* cities in the world.
3 That laptop is the *more / most* expensive in the shop.
4 Madrid is *higher / highest* than other capital cities in Europe.
5 My maths teacher is the *most good / best* in the school.
6 I think Paris is *more / most* beautiful than London.

4 Put the words in the correct order to make sentences.

0 river / longest / the / in / world / is / the
The Nile *is the longest river in the world.*
1 the / footballer / in / exciting / league / the / is / most
Messi _____
2 runner / world / 2017 / fastest / in / the / was / the / in
Usain Bolt _____
3 most / class / computer / the / our / is / popular / game / in
FIFA Football _____
4 chocolate / has / hot / my / the / best / town / in
That café _____

5 Correct the mistakes in the sentences.

👁 1 It was the great holiday ever.
2 You should go to the MetroCentre because it's the big shopping centre in the UK.
3 You can wear your older clothes for this job.
4 The easier subject at school is PE.
5 The most expensive cost £900 and the cheaper cost £400.

1 What can you do online? Complete the table with the words in the box. Some words can go in more than one column.

FAMILY VIDEOS MUSIC SHOES
WEBSITES FRIENDS
PICTURES FILMS CLOTHES

buy	chat to	download	visit	watch

2 Complete the sentences with the words in the box.

digital   machines   memory
save   software   virus

1 I have a lot of photos on my phone so the _____ is almost full.
2 Did you remember to _____ your work before you turned the computer off?
3 My father has a new _____ camera. It takes great photos.
4 The school computers have got a _____ so they don't work very well.
5 My mum loves technology and we have a lot of _____ in our house.
6 My school uses special _____ for sending messages to parents and students.

1 What can we use very small computers for? Choose the best answer(s). Then read the magazine article and check your ideas.

A finding lost objects   **C** helping doctors
B watching films   **D** doing homework

The smallest computer in the world

Computers are smaller and smaller every day. The smallest computer in the world is like a grain of rice. It is only 2 mm long. It's called a micro-computer.

1 _____

Because they are useful for doing many different things. Doctors can put one inside a person's body and it can tell them the temperature of part of the body or it can take photos so they can see what is happening inside the body.

These micro-computers can also help us find things. Imagine you can't find your door key or your smartphone. You can put a micro-computer on your key or smartphone and the computer can tell you where your key is. Amazing!

2 _____

They use electricity made from light so they only need a very small battery and they are very cheap. They aren't heavy so you can put them anywhere you want, in clothes, in water or even on an animal.

3 _____

They don't have a screen or a printer, so when you want to look at pictures or print information, you connect them to a different machine. You can't watch films or use them for your homework either!

2 Read the article again and match the questions to the paragraphs (1–3).

A What is good about these computers?
B What is the problem with these computers?
C Why do people want very small computers?

LISTENING

1 You will hear Matt talking to his friend Sara about a technology festival. For each question, choose the correct answer.

1 The Technology Festival is in
   A the shopping centre.   **B** the library.   **C** the station.

2 Sara saw a robot
   A online.   **B** at home.   **C** in class.

3 How much does the festival cost?
   A £6   **B** £8   **C** £10

4 Last year Matt bought a
   A camera.   **B** mouse.   **C** computer game.

5 Matt and Sarah are going to meet at
   A 10.45   **B** 11.00   **C** 12.00

1 Match the questions to the answers.

1 Would you like to go to a concert? ....
2 Where is the concert? ....
3 How much does it cost? ....
4 How can we get there? ....
5 Which band is playing in the concert? ....
6 What time does it finish? ....

a There's a bus.
b It's a rock singer called James.
c It's in the old cinema.
d About 10 o'clock, I think.
e I'd love to go.
f £10

2 Put the words in the correct order to make questions.

1 Saturday / are / busy / on / you / ?

2 on / are / what / you / Sunday / doing / ?

3 Friday / you / to / would / go / swimming / like / on / ?

4 afternoon / you / to / do / go / this / to / the / want / park / ?

3 Read the email. Match the words and phrases in **bold** in the email to the words and phrases below.

> ¹ **Hi** Kim,
>
> ² **How are you?** Are you ³ **busy** on Sunday?
> ⁴ **Do you want** to go to the cinema with me on Sunday afternoon? ⁵ **I want** to watch the new film about robots and eat a burger.
>
> ⁶ **Love** Dana

a See you soon ....
b Dear ....
c I'd like ....

d Would you like ....
e no free time ....
f How are things? ....

4 Imagine you want to go to a technology festival with your English friend, Lenny. Write an email to Lenny. In the email:

- **ask** Lenny **to go to the festival with you** on Saturday.
- say **where** the festival is.
- say **what** you want to do there.

Write 25 words or more.

....
....
....
....
....
....

13 HEALTHY BODIES

VOCABULARY Illness

1 Put the letters in *italics* in the correct order to complete the sentences.

1 Jason can't play tennis because he's got a *nkerbo* _____ arm.
2 My mum had a *dcehaaeh* _____ so she stayed at home.
3 I need to go to the dentist because I've got *tocaothhe* _____.
4 I can't eat because I've got a *moahcts heca* _____.
5 I've got a *ldoc* _____ today so I'm going to stay at home.
6 My ears *rtuh* _____ because it's so cold.
7 She ate a lot of cake and now she feels *iskc* _____.
8 My sister's got a *pmetaerrute* _____ so she's in bed.
9 Did you have a *npia* _____ in your arm after you fell?

2 Complete the sentences with words in Exercise 1.

1 **A:** Do you want to go swimming this afternoon?
   B: Sorry, I can't. I've got _____. I think I need to go to the dentist.
2 OK. Let's see. Oh! 37.5 degrees! You've got a high _____.
3 **A:** What's the matter?
   B: I feel _____ and I've got a _____. I think I ate something bad.
4 **A:** Why are you walking slowly?
   B: I've got a _____ in my foot.
5 **A:** Does your arm _____ when I touch it?
   B: Ow! Yes.
   A: I think you've got a _____ arm.

3 Choose the correct words to complete the sentences.

1 I went to the doctor because I had a _____ in my stomach.
   A hurt   **B** pain   **C** sick
2 Your head feels hot. Have you got _____?
   A a temperature **B** toothache   **C** a cold
3 I can't play rugby for six weeks because I've got a _____.
   A stomach ache   **B** headache   **C** broken arm
4 I don't want to eat anything because I _____ sick.
   A get   **B** feel   **C** have

GRAMMAR should / shouldn't

1 Choose the correct words to complete the sentences.

To be healthy …
1 you *should / shouldn't* sleep eight or nine hours every night.
2 you *should / shouldn't* drink lots of water.
3 you *should / shouldn't* go to bed late.
4 you *should / shouldn't* exercise four or five times a week.
5 you *should / shouldn't* eat too much chocolate or cake.
6 you *should / shouldn't* eat lots of fish, fruit and vegetables.

2 Complete the sentences with the phrases in the box.

> eat so much chocolate   go to bed
> drink lots of water   study hard tonight
> sit down   play tennis this afternoon

1 **A:** I've got a pain in my right arm.
   B: You shouldn't
   ....

2 **A:** I'm very tired and it's late.
   B: Then you should
   ...., Sam.

3 **A:** My foot hurts.
   B: You should ....
   for a while.

4 **A:** I feel sick.
   B: Well, you shouldn't
   .... !

5 **A:** I've got a difficult maths exam
   tomorrow.
   B: You should ....

6 **A:** Sarah's got a terrible cold.
   B: She should rest and
   ....

3 Read the sentences. Is the advice right (✓) or wrong (✗)?

To improve your English …
0 you should read books in English.   ✓
1 you shouldn't talk to people from
   English-speaking countries.   ....
2 you should listen to music in English.   ....
3 you should watch films in English.   ....
4 you shouldn't practise pronunciation.   ....
5 you should only study at weekends.   ....

4 Correct the mistakes in three of the sentences. Which two are correct?

1 I think you shoud take a coat.

2 I should bring a DVD?

3 How much money should we bring?

4 You won't eat sweets in class. It's a school rule.

5 You will bring some water. It's very hot today.

6 Don't forget your keys. You should put them in your pocket.

1 Complete the blog with the phrases in the box.

> do some exercises   eat well   enter a race
> stay healthy   get fit   have a rest   sleep well

FITNESS FOR EVERYONE

Hi, everyone. Today I've got eight tips and pieces of advice for people who want to start running. Read on if you want to
1 .... in no time at all!

> Start slowly. Run a little, then
  2 ...., then run again.
> Run five times a week.
> 3 .... – lots of fruit and vegetables. A good diet helps you
  4 ....
> Drink lots of water.
> Don't watch screens late at night so you can 5 .... – eight hours a night at least.
> In bad weather you can
  6 .... in a gym.
> Remember, at first it hurts but later you feel great!
> 7 .... This will give you something to work towards in the future. Maybe you'll win!

2 Match the sentence halves.

1 It is very   ....
2 I like running but I don't want   ....
3 I try to keep fit so   ....
4 Swimming is a good way   ....
5 The secret to eating well   ....

a I go cycling, swimming and running.
b to stay healthy.
c to enter a race.
d important to do exercise.
e is lots of fruit and vegetables.

3 Choose the correct words to complete the sentences.

1 I like to *get* / *keep* some exercise when I'm on holiday.
2 You should *do* / *have* a rest after so much running.
3 She's going to the gym because she wants to *get* / *have* fit.
4 You *do* / *feel* healthy when you eat well.
5 I'm going to *get* / *enter* the 100 m race in the school sports day.
6 You should *do* / *take* some exercises to make your legs stronger.

1 Read the article and tick (✓) the sports that are mentioned.

1 baseball	....	**4** running	....	**7** snowboarding	....
2 cycling	....	**5** skateboarding	....	**8** surfing	....
3 football	....	**6** skating	....	**9** swimming	....

THE FITTEST
member of my family

My cousin Alex is 18 years old. She runs three kilometres every morning before school, she cycles to school, she swims in the school swimming pool at lunchtime and then she cycles home after school. Can you believe it?

That's not all! On Saturdays she enters races. These are special events called 'triathlons'. In triathlons, the athletes have to swim, cycle and run a very long way. Alex is very good at triathlons. Last year, she won six events, finished second three times and third four times. Alex wants to be in the Olympics when she's older.

Do you want to keep fit? Alex has lots of good advice. 'Don't think about it, don't talk about it, just do it. Oh, and don't do any exercise on Sundays. Have a rest that day. I always do. It's very important to have a rest.'

I'd like to be as fit as Alex but I can't run fast and I'm not good at swimming. However, I am good at skateboarding. Maybe I'll go to the Olympics … but only to watch my cousin!

2 Read the article again and answer the questions. Write complete sentences.

1 How does Alex get to school? ....
2 What does she do at lunchtime? ....
3 What does she do on Saturdays? ....
4 How many triathlons did she win last year? ....
5 What does she want to do when she is older? ....
6 When does she have a rest? ....

LISTENING

🔊 **1** Listen to four conversations. Match the conversations (1–4) to the places (A–D).

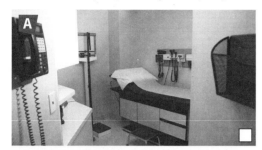

A ☐

B ☐

C ☐

D ☐

🔊 **2** Listen to the conversations again. Are the sentences right (✓) or wrong (✗)?

1 William hasn't got a headache. ....
2 Susie has got a pain in her arm. ....
3 Carla's eye hurts. ....
4 Marek's foot hurts. ....
5 Marek thinks his hand is broken. ....

🔊 **3** Complete the sentences from the conversations with the words in the box. Then listen again and check your answers.

about	matter	should	wrong

1 You _____ take some medicine.
2 What's the _____, Susie?
3 OK, Carla. Tell me, what's
   _____?
4 What _____ your hand?

WRITING — An email giving advice

1 Read the email from Emily to her penfriend Jacob. What does Emily want?

_____

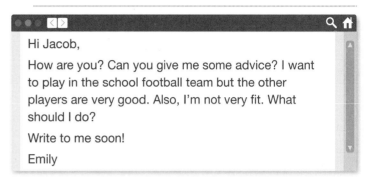

Hi Jacob,

How are you? Can you give me some advice? I want to play in the school football team but the other players are very good. Also, I'm not very fit. What should I do?

Write to me soon!

Emily

2 Complete Jacob's answer to Emily's email with the words in the box.

exercise	football	gym
healthy	park	running

Hi Emily,

I think you should do some [1] _____. You should go [2] _____ every day and go to the [3] _____ in the sports centre. You need to practise [4] _____ so you should go to the [5] _____ and play with your friends. You should also eat [6] _____ food, like fish and vegetables!

Jacob

3 Read Jacob's email again and answer the questions.

1 How often should Emily go running? _____
2 Where should she go in the sports centre? _____
3 Who should she play football with? _____
4 What should she eat? _____

4 Read the email from your friend Harry. Write an answer to him. Write about 50 words.

Hi,

How are you? Can you help me? I broke my leg last month but now it's better. I want to get fit again. What should I do?

Harry

Hi Harry,

_____
_____
_____
_____
_____
_____

14 GETTING AROUND TOWN

VOCABULARY Places in town

1 Put the letters in the correct order to make town words.

1 b r i a y r l ....
2 t c r f a f i   i g t l s h ....
3 g i r b d e s ....
4 s b u   s o p t s ....
5 t e s e t s r ....
6 r u d a o b o t n u ....

2 Match the words to the definitions.

1 These change colour from red and yellow
to green when the cars can go. ....

2 You can buy fruit and vegetables here. ....

3 People and cars can use this to go across
a river or a road. ....

4 This is round and several roads meet here. ....

5 This is where students at school go at break time. ....

6 You can read books here. ....

a bridge
b library
c roundabout
d traffic lights
e playground
f market

3 Choose the correct words to complete the sentences.

1 My mother went to the *police / petrol* station to put air into her car's tyres.
2 I took the letter to the *post / message* office.
3 My friends and I play volleyball at the sports *centre / station*.
4 There is a very long *shopping / street* in the middle of the town.
5 A lot of buses go from the bus *centre / station* to other cities.
6 I go to a swimming *station / pool* near my house twice a week.

GRAMMAR Prepositions

1 Look at the map and choose the correct prepositions to complete the sentences.

1 The museum is *next to / opposite* the park.
2 The football stadium is *next to / through* the car park.
3 The car park is *through / in front of* the train station.
4 The restaurant is *beside / in front of* the cinema.
5 The post office is *opposite / beside* the restaurant.

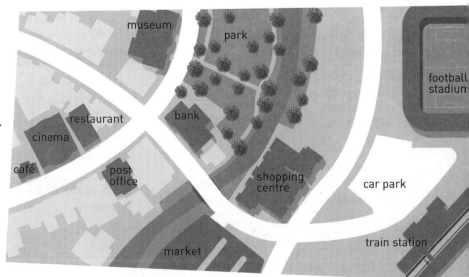

2 Look at the map on page 60 again and complete the sentences. Sometimes more than one answer is possible.

1 The football stadium is _____ the town.
2 The cinema is _____ the café.
3 The restaurant is _____ the post office.
4 The bank is _____ the park.
5 There is a river going _____ the town.
6 There is a bridge _____ the river.
7 There is a market _____ the shopping centre.

3 Complete the conversations with the words in the box.

after	go	near	next
on	turn	way	where

1 **A:** Excuse me, which [1] _____ is the library?
  B: Go straight [2] _____ . The library is on your left.
2 **A:** Is there a post office [3] _____ here?
  B: Yes, there is. [4] _____ left at the roundabout. The post office is on your right.
3 **A:** Excuse me, [5] _____ is the bank?
  B: It's opposite the cinema. [6] _____ past the supermarket and it's on your left.
4 **A:** Excuse me, is there a petrol station near here?
  B: Umm, yes, there's one [7] _____ to the shopping centre. Drive along this street and turn right at the bridge. It's there just [8] _____ the park.
  A: Thank you very much.

4 Choose the correct words to complete the sentences.

1 The school is *between / next to* the bus station.
2 I live opposite the *supermarket / street*.
3 We can meet *out of / outside* my house.
4 Go *through / along* the main street.
5 The lake has a bridge *across / under* it.

VOCABULARY Compound nouns

1 Match the two parts of the compound nouns.

1 guide	_____	**a** card
2 post	_____	**b** tour
3 walking	_____	**c** coat
4 tour	_____	**d** book
5 rain	_____	**e** tour
6 cycle	_____	**f** guide

2 Match the compound nouns in Exercise 1 to the definitions.

1 This has information for tourists. It tells them about places to visit.
 _____
2 You can write on this and send it to a friend.
 _____
3 This is when you look around a small town on foot.
 _____
4 This person shows you the best places to visit.
 _____
5 You wear this when the weather is bad.
 _____
6 This is when you visit different places on a bike.
 _____

3 Complete the text with compound nouns in Exercise 1.

Last summer I went on a [1] _____ in Italy with my parents and my younger sister – a wonderful weekend enjoying the Italian countryside on foot!. We went to Bergamo where we met our [2] _____ . She gave us a [3] _____ to look at on the way. Then we caught a bus to the mountains. Two hours later the bus stopped near a river. It was sunny and warm so we didn't need a [4] _____ . We walked past lakes, through villages and over mountains. It was very beautiful. In one village we found a very small shop and I bought a [5] _____ to send to my best friend.

a great place for a
family
day!

1 Read the magazine article about a model village and tick (✓) the places you can find there.

1 a train station ....
2 a castle ....
3 a beach ....
4 a cinema ....

5 a zoo ....
6 a museum ....
7 a mountain ....

Bekonscot Model Village is nearly 90 years old. It's the oldest model village in the world and it's amazing. There are lots of different things to see there. They all look real but of course they are very small!

One place is a zoo with model giraffes and chimpanzees. There are model people looking at the animals in the zoo. Another place is a town next to the sea with a beach. Model children are playing in the water and other people are walking on the sand. There are streets where you can see cars and buses and traffic lights. The traffic lights change colour and the cars move! The main street has lots of shops – with model people inside the shops and on the street. You can look in the shops and see what they are selling.

There is a train station next to the town with little trains that go around the village, across bridges or through tunnels. There is also a mountain and you can watch people climbing it. My favourite place is the castle. It has a king and queen – they are standing at the entrance waving.

You can stay in the model village all morning and then have lunch in a café next to the village. The food is very good – it's real food!

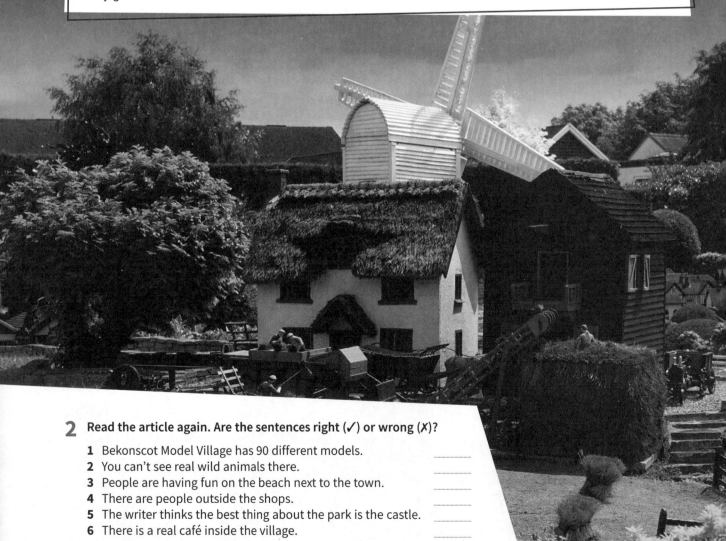

2 Read the article again. Are the sentences right (✓) or wrong (✗)?

1 Bekonscot Model Village has 90 different models. ....
2 You can't see real wild animals there. ....
3 People are having fun on the beach next to the town. ....
4 There are people outside the shops. ....
5 The writer thinks the best thing about the park is the castle. ....
6 There is a real café inside the village. ....

🔊 **1** You will hear Lucas talking to a friend about his trip to Cardiff with his family. Which place did each person visit on Saturday?

People
0 Lucas   `E`
1 sister   ☐
2 mum   ☐
3 brother   ☐
4 dad   ☐
5 grandfather   ☐

Places
A castle
B cinema
C clothes shop
D park
E museum
F restaurant
G theatre
H stadium

WRITING   An article

1 Write *this* or *these*.

1 _____ buildings
2 _____ streets
3 _____ river
4 _____ park
5 _____ museums
6 _____ cinema

2 Choose the correct words to complete the text.

Budapest is the capital of Hungary and it's in the centre of Europe. ¹ *This / These* city is one of the most beautiful in the world. The River Danube goes through the city. On one side of ² *this / these* river there is the old part of the city. It's called Buda. There are many lovely old buildings there. ³ *This / These* are very popular with tourists. On the other side is the new part of the city called Pest. There are lots of cinemas there. ⁴ *This / These* cinemas show lots of interesting films. Margaret Island is a very interesting place in Budapest. It's in the middle of the Danube in the centre of the city. ⁵ *This / These* island has parks, tennis courts and swimming pools.

3 Complete the article with the words and phrases in the box.

| lovely beaches   young people and families |
| a lot of shops   beautiful   the museum |
| it has an old photograph of my street |
| sell clothes and food   Galicia, in Spain |

My town is in ¹ _____.
It is a ² _____
place. Near the town there are lots of
³ _____. These are
popular with ⁴ _____.
In the town centre there are
⁵ _____. These
⁶ _____.
An interesting place in my town is
⁷ _____. I like it
because ⁸ _____.

4 Write an article about your town or city. Use the text in Exercise 3 to help you and write about 50 words. Remember to use *this* and *these* correctly.

_____
_____
_____
_____
_____

VOCABULARY Geographical features

1 Put the letters in *italics* in the correct order to make words about size.

1 The school bus is 9 metres *goln*. ....
2 The river in the town is 20 metres *dwei*. ....
3 The swimming pool is 2 metres *epde*. ....
4 The Eiffel Tower is 324 metres *gihh*. ....

2 Complete the sentences with the words in Exercise 1.

1 We walked along Yonge Street in Toronto, but we couldn't walk along all of it because it's 86 kilometres ....
2 My brother and his friends climbed Denali in Alaska. It's 6,190 metres ....
3 We went to the Grand Canyon on our holiday to North America. It wasn't easy to see the bottom. It's about 1,800 metres .... !
4 My friends and I wanted to swim across Lake Ontario, but it's 85 kilometres .... !

3 Label the picture with the words in the box.

| cliff | field | island |
| lake | mountain | river |

4 Choose the correct words to complete the sentences.

1 There are some cows *on the mountain* / *in the field*.
2 The *cliff* / *lake* is near the sea.
3 The river goes from the *field* / *lake* to the sea.
4 There are some trees on the *mountain* / *island*.
5 There is a bridge across the *lake* / *river*.
6 There is *water* / *snow* on the mountains.

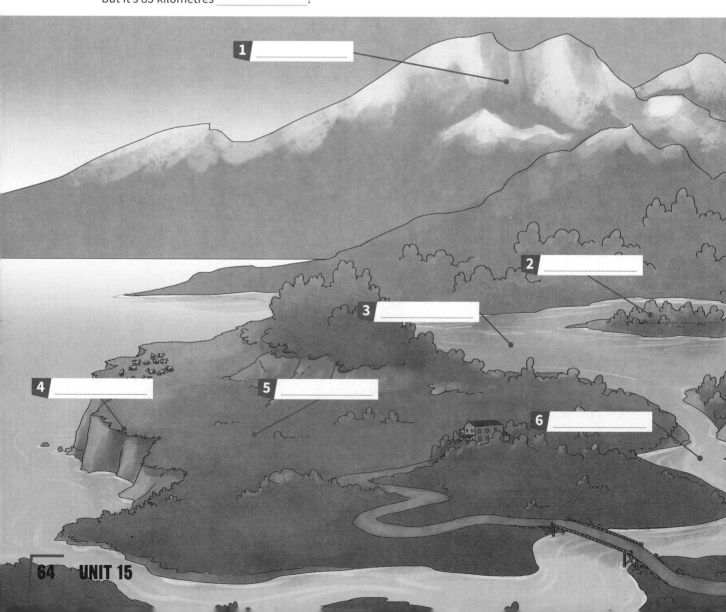

Past continuous

1 Look at the picture and correct the sentences below.

0 Mr and Mrs Roberts were eating pizza.
They weren't eating pizza. They were making pizza.
1 Caitlin was doing her homework.

2 Jack was playing the piano.

3 Toby was reading a magazine.

4 Chloe and Harry were playing football.

5 Grandma Roberts was standing up.

2 Write questions in the past continuous.

0 Michael / watch / TV last night / ?
Was Michael watching TV last night?
1 he / help / his / parents / ?

2 Tia and Karl / swim / in the sea / ?

3 they / do / their homework / ?

4 your friend / play / volleyball / ?

5 you / read / a book / ?

3 Complete the short answers.

0 Was Mia doing her homework last night?
Yes, *she was* .
1 Were Katie and Alex having lunch at 2 o'clock?
No, .
2 Were you reading a book in class today?
Yes, .
3 Was Mrs Brown writing on the board?
No, .
4 Were they sleeping at midnight?
Yes, .
5 Was William eating an ice cream?
No, .

4 Correct the mistakes in three of the sentences. Which two are correct?

1 I was enjoying my birthday party last week.

2 What were you doing yesterday at 4 pm?

3 I went to the cinema yesterday.

4 I liked it because was playing my favourite team.

5 When we were on holiday, we were swimming every day.

The weather

1 Write the nouns of the weather words.

0	cloudy	*cloud*	**4**	snowy	
1	foggy		**5**	sunny	
2	icy		**6**	windy	
3	rainy				

2 Complete the sentences with nouns and adjectives in Exercise 1.

1 We often go snowboarding when there is _____ in the mountains.
2 It's very _____ in the north of Europe so take your umbrella when you go there.
3 The street is very _____ because the temperature is –1 °C, so walk carefully!
4 There was a lot of _____ so I couldn't see the end of the garden from my window.
5 I love _____ weather when I can go to the beach and swim.

1 Read this strange story quickly. How did the two girls meet?

Strange stories

Many years ago, when she was nearly ten years old, Laura Buxton was playing in the garden with a balloon. Her family were having a party. She wrote a message on the balloon: 'Please return to Laura Buxton' and her address. It was a windy day and suddenly the balloon flew out of her hand and into the sky. This balloon travelled more than 200 km until it came down near the garden of another little girl. A man found the balloon, read the message and took it to her house. This girl was very surprised to see the message because her name was Laura Buxton too! And she was just ten years old.

The second Laura wrote a letter to the first Laura and then their parents telephoned so they could meet. When they met, the girls noticed that they were both wearing pink jumpers and jeans, both girls were also tall and thin and had long brown hair and brown eyes. They were amazed! They talked and found they had the same pets – a three-year-old black dog, a grey rabbit and a guinea pig. They became good friends. Now they are older and they are still friends. They are waiting for more magic to happen!

2 Read the story again and number the events in the order they happened.

a The girls noticed they were wearing the same clothes. ....

b Laura One was playing with a balloon. *1*

c A man gave Laura Two the balloon. ....

d The wind blew the balloon away. ....

e The girls are friends now. ....

f Laura Two wrote to Laura One. ....

g A man found the balloon. ....

h The girls went to meet each other. ....

LISTENING

🔊 **1** Listen to the conversation about Jack's holiday and
15   tick (✓) the activities his family did.

1 go swimming _____   5 go shopping _____
2 go to the beach _____   6 go to a restaurant _____
3 play games _____   7 go skiing _____
4 go on a boat _____

🔊 **2** Listen again and match the days to the weather.
15

1 Saturday _____   a snowy
2 Sunday _____   b rainy
3 Monday _____   c cloudy
4 Tuesday _____   d windy
5 Wednesday _____   e sunny
6 Thursday _____   f foggy

WRITING   A description or story about a strange animal

1 Match the questions about an animal to the answers.

1 Which country does the animal live in? _____   a It comes out at night to walk in the town.
2 Where does the animal live? _____   b It is called the Bondar.
3 What does it look like? _____   c It lives in the forest.
4 What does it do? _____   d It is short and fat with lots of hair.
5 What is it called? _____   e It lives in Russia.
6 Is it real or not? _____   f It's not real.

2 Put the words in the correct order to make sentences.

1 people / town / in / scared / the / were / the

_____

2 living / the / forest / was / the / Bondar / in

_____

3 he / a / went / one / to / house / night

_____

4 boy / food / gave / a / him / some / little

_____

5 became / boy / the / friends / the / Bondar / with

_____

3 Complete the text with the words in the box.

big   forest   hair   lives   mountains   saw

BIGFOOT is a strange animal. This animal ¹ _____ in the United States.
It is very tall, it has a lot of ² _____ and very ³ _____ feet. It lives
in wild places, maybe in high ⁴ _____ called the Rockies. It walks around
the countryside looking for food. Some people say they ⁵ _____ Bigfoot.
It was walking through a ⁶ _____ near a river. I don't think it is real!

4 Find out about a strange animal and write a description or story about it. Use the
questions in Exercise 1 to help you and write about 50 words.

_____
_____
_____
_____

16 AMAZING ANIMALS

VOCABULARY Animals

1 Use the photos to complete the crossword.

Across

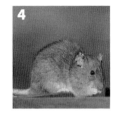

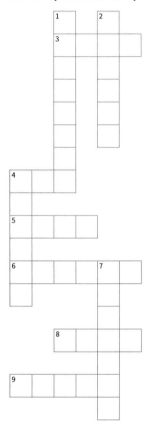

Down

2 Complete the word clouds with words in Exercise 1.

1 six legs

2 two legs

3 can fly

4 big ears

5 popular pets

6 carnivore

3 Choose the correct words to complete the sentences.

1 There are more *elephants / insects* in the world than any other animal.
2 A *duck / lion* can fly.
3 A *chicken / bear* is a wild animal.
4 You can find *chickens / monkeys* on a farm.
5 You can keep *a mouse / an elephant* as a pet in your house.
6 *Rats / Bears* live in the city and in the countryside.

GRAMMAR — Past simple and past continuous

1 Match the sentence halves.

1 The girl was playing basketball
2 My parents were waiting for me
3 My cousin fell off his bike
4 When the teacher came back to the class,
5 While the boy was making a sandwich,
6 While the man was walking his dog,

a he cut his finger.
b all the students were talking.
c when she fell and hurt her arm.
d he found €20 in the street.
e while he was cycling round the park.
f at the airport when I got off the plane.

2 Complete the sentences with the past simple or past continuous form of the verbs in brackets.

1 We _____ (play) tennis when it _____ (start) to rain.
2 I _____ (walk) through the park when I _____ (find) a wallet.
3 Jo _____ (watch) TV when I _____ (call) her.
4 What _____ (you / do) yesterday afternoon at 3 pm?
5 I _____ (buy) Mum's birthday present while I _____ (shop) with my friends.
6 While we _____ (wait) for the bus, my brother _____ (drive) past.

3 Complete the sentences with *when* or *while*.

1 He was snowboarding _____ he fell and broke his leg.
2 _____ I was sitting on the bus, I saw my English teacher.
3 She learned a lot of English _____ she was living in London.
4 _____ I got home I went into the kitchen.

4 Choose the correct verb form to complete the sentences.

1 I felt very nervous while I _____ the game.
  A watched   B was watching
2 When I saw them, I _____ in love.
  A fell   B was falling
3 While we _____ around the castle, we saw a very old picture.
  A looked   B were looking
4 Yesterday, while I _____ back home, I remembered I left my sunglasses in your house.
  A came   B was coming
5 When I _____ in the kitchen, I saw a broken window.
  A cleaned   B was cleaning

VOCABULARY — Phrasal verbs

1 Complete the sentences with the past simple form of the phrasal verbs in the box.

get on	get off	turn on
turn off	pick up	look after

1 Jenny _____ the TV and did her homework.
2 Tom _____ the bus and sat near the front.
3 Jack _____ the rabbit when Lisa was on holiday.
4 Debbie _____ the train and walked home.
5 Paula _____ the laptop and wrote an email.
6 Amon _____ the book and put it on the shelf.

2 Choose the correct words to complete the sentences.

1 When she finished her homework, she turned the computer *on / off* and went to bed.
2 Freddy got *off / on* the bus at the wrong bus stop and had to walk a long way.
3 Finally, we got *on / off* the plane and found our seats.
4 Don't leave those papers on the floor. Pick them *up / out* and put them on the table.
5 Can you look *for / after* my pet mouse when I go away on holiday?
6 Please turn *off / on* your phone before you go into the cinema.

READING

1 Read the story about Kylie and her dog and answer the questions.

One morning, Kylie, her father and their dog, Lua, went for a walk in the mountains. Kylie was only four years old but she could walk very well. Her father stopped to take a photo of a bird. He finished and looked around, but Kylie and Lua weren't there. When he called Kylie's name, she didn't answer. Her father was afraid because maybe Kylie was hurt. He phoned the police and lots of people started looking for the little girl. After seven hours, when it was nearly night time, they found her. She was in the forest four kilometres away. They found her because Lua was making a noise. Kylie was sleeping with Lua, and Lua was keeping her warm. Her amazing pet was staying with her to protect her.

1 How old was Kylie? ....

2 What was her father doing when Kylie got lost? ....

3 Where was Kylie when they found her? ....

4 How did they find her? ....

5 Why wasn't Kylie cold? ....

2 For each question, choose the correct answer.

Bats

Bats are very special animals. They are not birds, [1] .... they can fly. Bats often live in trees. They [2] .... very thin wings and can fly very quickly. Bats sleep in the day and come out [3] .... night. They usually eat insects and can eat thousands of them. One bat can eat about 1,200 insects in one hour.

Many people think that bats can't see, but that isn't true. Bats can see, but their ears are [4] .... important to them than their eyes. [5] .... people are afraid of bats, but bats are not dangerous animals.

Bats sometimes fly into people's houses. [6] .... this happens, you should open all the windows. The bat will soon fly out again.

1 A but	**B** so	**C** or	
2 A had	**B** has	**C** have	
3 A in	**B** at	**C** on	

4 A much	**B** most	**C** more	
5 A Some	**B** Any	**C** All	
6 A When	**B** And	**C** While	

LISTENING

◁)) 16 1 Listen to the conversation between Kirsty and Donny and answer the questions.

1 Which is Kirsty's favourite pet?
....

2 Which animal would Kirsty like to have? ....

◁)) 16 2 Listen again and match the animals to the numbers.

1 five	....	**a** monkeys
2 twelve	....	**b** horses
3 nine	....	**c** dogs
4 two	....	**d** cats
5 seven	....	**e** rabbits

◁)) 16 3 Listen again. Are the sentences right (✓) or wrong (✗)?

1 Kirsty has got 24 animals. ....

2 Kirsty has got some birds. ....

3 Kirsty loves her pet rat very much. ....

4 Kirsty's garden is very big. ....

5 Kirsty had some monkeys in the past. ....

6 Donny wants to see one of her animals. ....

1 Look at the three pictures. Then complete 1–8 in the text below with the past simple or past continuous form of the verbs in brackets.

(A) *Then / One day* at school, **(B)** *while / then* the teacher ¹ _____ (draw) an elephant on the board, Paul ² _____ (see) a monkey in a tree outside. He ³ _____ (go) to the window and ⁴ _____ (open) it. **(C)** *While / Then* the monkey ⁵ _____ (come) inside and ⁶ _____ (sit) down. **(D)** *Finally, / One day*, the teacher ⁷ _____ (see) the monkey. She ⁸ _____ (be) very surprised and the students started laughing.

2 Choose the correct words and phrases (A–D) to complete the text.

3 Look at the pictures and answer the questions below.

1 What was the weather like?
_____

2 What were the girls doing?
_____

3 What did the girl see?
_____

4 What did the kite do?
_____

5 What did the boy probably say to the girls?
_____

6 How did the girls help the boy?
_____

4 Write the story shown in the pictures in Exercise 3. Write 35 words or more. Remember to use *one day*, *then*, *while* and *finally*.

_____
_____
_____
_____
_____
_____
_____

AMAZING ANIMALS 71

17 WHAT ARE YOU WATCHING?

VOCABULARY   Television

1 Match the sentence halves.

1 You can use the remote control ....
2 I like to watch the news ....
3 I watched a great talent show ....
4 I'm not a fan of ....
5 I use my computer to stream ....
6 I prefer to watch live football games ....

a on TV last night.
b cartoons for children but I sometimes watch them with my little sister.
c on an American channel like CNN.
d than record them for later.
e programmes I don't have time to watch live.
f to change channels on the TV.

2 Choose the correct words to complete the sentences.

1 My mother is the biggest *talent* / *fan* of Rafa Nadal. She watches all his matches.
2 He couldn't watch the *live* / *direct* concert but he saw it the next day.
3 My favourite *channel* / *cartoon* is Nickelodeon.
4 I can't find the *distance* / *remote* control to turn the TV on.
5 You can use the internet to *record* / *stream* lots of programmes from other countries.
6 Our TV is so old we can't watch anything on *demand* / *screen*, only what they are showing at the time you turn it on.
7 I was surprised to see my best friend on the *news* / *talent show* last night. She was talking about a sports competition in our town.

3 Complete the sentences with the words in the box.

| demand | fan | live | programmes |
| stream | talent show | | |

1 The .... was on TV very late last night so I'm going to .... it this evening.
2 My brother's a big .... of basketball. He always watches the matches ....
3 I like to watch films on .... when I finish my homework because there are never any other good .... on at that time.

GRAMMAR   Future with *going to*

1 Look at the photos. What are the people going to do? Complete the sentences with the correct form of *going to*.

1 He ....

2 She ....

3 They ....

4 He ....

5 She ....

2 Write sentences with *going to*.

1 He / not / finish his lunch

2 I / visit my mum in hospital

3 She / not / phone her friend

4 We / invite our friends to the party

5 They / not / stream the film

6 We / not / go to the concert

3 Correct the mistakes in four of the sentences. Which two are correct?

1 She's going to meet us on Saturday afternoon.

2 I go to play tennis and football.

3 I'm happy because you going to come to my house.

4 They're going to travel around South America.

5 We going to get to the sports centre by car.

6 I hope you go have a lovely time in my town.

4 Connect the questions, answers and comments.

1 Are you going to watch the news tonight?
2 Is he going to make a cake?
3 Are they going to play volleyball this Saturday?
4 Are you going to walk home after school today?

Yes, he is.
Yes, we are.
No, I'm not.
No, they aren't.

There are no games this weekend.
I'm going to go to bed early.
Do you want to come with us?
It's for his mother's birthday.

VOCABULARY   Entertainment

1 Put the letters in *italics* in the correct order to make words about talent shows.

TALENT 100

Welcome to the first programme of **Talent 100**! In the [1] *disuto* tonight we have ten artists for the first [2] *tipcmoenoti*. Each [3] *mefporrer* has five minutes to show us their talent: singing, dancing or playing a musical instrument. We also have our experts – Lisa Minne won last year and she is back to be a [4] *gejdu* with Steve and Kathy. We also ask the [5] *iedacuen* to give their thoughts. Everyone can [6] *evto orf* their favourite act online or by phone. This year there are going to be ten shows. The [7] *newnri* of each show will go to [8] *het alnfi* in May. The first [9] *rzepi* is going to be £10,000 and the [10] *nruren-pu* is going to get £3,000. But first, on the [11] *atges* tonight we have a famous [12] *rast* – Adele – who is going to sing her new song.

2 Match the words in the box to the meanings.

audience	judge	runner-up	stage	star	studio	winner

1 This person gets first prize.

2 This person gets second prize.

3 Performers stand here when they sing or dance.

4 This person chooses the best performer.

5 This is a very famous performer.

6 A talent show is recorded here.

7 These people watch a talent show.

1 Read Tom's blog. Where does he live?

....

Tom's Cartoon BLOG

I like watching cartoons very much. My favourite cartoon is *The Simpsons*. It's very funny. *The Simpsons* is a famous American TV programme and I am a very big fan of it. It's the story of a family in a small town in the United States. Homer and Marge are the parents of three children, Bart, Lisa and Maggie. Lisa is my favourite because she's very clever, but Bart is fun too. Maggie is a baby. She doesn't talk at all.

In the UK, you can watch *The Simpsons* on Channel Four. It's on TV every night. I often watch it with my brother and sister. We can also watch every programme on demand and we like to watch them again and again. I sometimes stream episodes on my tablet because I have homework in the evening, so I watch them when I finish, or the next day.

Last week, I had a big surprise. I met Lisa Simpson! Yes, really! My mum has a Spanish friend and she came to visit us at home in England. She's an actress and her job is doing the voice of Lisa Simpson in Spanish. My mum's friend is an adult, but she can speak with a little girl's voice. It was very funny to listen to her! I think Spanish children like *The Simpsons* the same as I do.

2 Read the blog again and answer the questions.

1 What country is *The Simpsons* from? ....
2 What type of TV programme is *The Simpsons*? ....
3 Who are Marge and Homer? ....
4 How many children are there in *The Simpsons*? ....
5 What two machines does Tom watch *The Simpsons* on? ....
6 Where did Tom meet the actress who does Lisa Simpson's voice? ....
7 What kind of voice does Tom's mum's friend use for her job? ....
8 Can you watch *The Simpsons* in Spanish? ....

LISTENING

🔊 17 **1** Listen to an interview with Josie. What are her plans for the future?

....

🔊 17 **2** Listen again and answer the questions.

1 Why is Josie famous?

2 Where did she work in the past?

3 What does her boyfriend do?

4 What did she win in the competition?

5 What is she going to do first?

6 What does she think is the most important thing a good cook needs to do?

WRITING | A text about a talent show

1 Read the text and answer the questions.

1 What's the name of the show?

2 How many judges are there?

3 Who won the competition?

4 What band does Jenna like?

5 Do other people like the show?

2 Think about a talent show you like and answer the questions.

1 What's the name of the show?

2 When can you see it?

3 What do people do in the show?

4 What are the names of some of the performers?

5 What do you like about them?

6 Is the show popular?

3 Write about your talent show. Use your answers to the questions in Exercise 2 and write about 50 words.

....

....

....

....

....

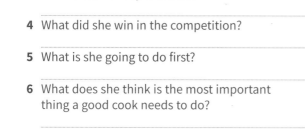

A GREAT SHOW

My name's Jenna. My favourite talent show is called *The Voice Kids*. It's live on TV on Tuesday nights. There are a lot of singers on the show and three famous judges. The best performer is a girl called Jess. She's 14 years old and she sings very well. She won an amazing holiday to Disneyland Paris. She also got to sing with my favourite band, The Vamps! All my friends watch this programme. I think it is very popular.

VOCABULARY Magazines

1 Match the words in the box to the pictures and photos.

> advertisement   cartoon   headline
> interview   photograph

1 _____

2 _____

3 _____

4 _____

5 _____

2 Match the type of writing to the examples.

1 an **article** about nature _____
2 a **headline** about a sports event _____
3 some **information** about a walking tour _____
4 an **interview** with a pop star _____
5 a **review** of a book _____

a It was really interesting and I recommend that everyone reads it.
b 'What are your plans for next year?' 'I'm going to give concerts in the USA.'
c You can find these animals in the Amazon rainforest.
d SPANISH TEAM WIN THE MATCH
e We will start at the market square at 10 am.

3 Complete the email from Harry to the headteacher of his school with the words in Exercises 1 and 2.

> **To:** headteacher@lytonschool.org
> **From:** Class 3B
> **Subject:** School magazine

Dear Mrs Young,

In Class 3B we are going to make a monthly school magazine. We saw an ¹_____ in the town newspaper last Monday for a competition and we want to enter. We have to include different sections. There is a page for a ²_____ of a film, a page with ³_____ about school activities, like sports matches or concerts, and a page for an ⁴_____ about any topic we want – perhaps something on the new school science lab? One of the students, Tess Williams, can draw very well, so she can draw a great ⁵_____ of our class! We would also like to include an ⁶_____ with you. Can I come to your office and ask you some questions? The ⁷_____ for this could be 'A DAY IN THE LIFE OF OUR HEADTEACHER'. We would like a ⁸_____ of you as well. Can we take one?

Thank you very much,

Harry Dawson (class 3B representative)

GRAMMAR — Making suggestions

1 Match the sentence halves.

1 Why don't we
2 Let's
3 Shall
4 Why not call

a we start a school magazine?
b watch the new cartoon on BBC 3 tonight?
c our online newspaper *The Buzz*?
d stop. I'm tired.

2 Complete the conversation with the words in the box.

| why   don't   let's   not   shall |

George: Hi, Alba. Are you free this weekend?
Alba: Yes, I am. ¹ _____ we meet in the city and go shopping?
George: Good idea. I need some new shoes. ² _____ not go to the new shopping centre next to the post office?
Alba: Excellent idea. It's got a great café. Why ³ _____ we have lunch there?
George: Yes, OK. And ⁴ _____ go to the cinema in the afternoon. I'd like to see the new James Bond film.
Alba: Hmm. I'd like to see the cartoon about the singing mouse.
George: OK. Why ⁵ _____ see both?
Alba: Great!

3 Write suggestions to make to a friend or family member for this weekend.

0 Let's *go skating this weekend.*
1 Why don't we _____ ?
2 Shall we _____ ?
3 Why not _____ ?
4 Let's _____ .
5 _____ .

4 <u>Underline</u> five mistakes with phrases for making suggestions in the email.

> To: Javi
> From: Marina
> Subject: Saturday
>
> Hi Javi,
>
> How are you? Thanks for your email. Yes, I'm free on Saturday. Lets go to the cinema! Why not seeing the new *Hidden Figures* film? Shall we to go to the cinema café before the film? They have great cakes! Why doesn't we meet in front of the cinema at 5 o'clock? Is that OK for you? Why not to call me tonight and we can talk about it?
>
> Speak soon,
>
> Marina

5 Correct the mistakes in the email in Exercise 4.

1 _____
2 _____
3 _____
4 _____
5 _____

VOCABULARY — *as, because, so* and *when*

1 Match the sentence halves.

1 I read a review of a film
2 I didn't go to the cinema
3 I bought a magazine to read
4 The book was great,

a when I got to the airport.
b so I think you should read it.
c because I wanted to know more about it.
d as I had no money.

2 Complete the sentences with the words in the box. Sometimes more than one answer is possible.

| as   because   so   when |

1 The school magazine is great _____ it has interesting articles.
2 The film was boring, _____ I fell asleep in the cinema.
3 _____ the singer finished performing, the audience stood up and applauded.
4 We didn't enjoy the beach _____ it was raining.
5 It's the cheapest shop in town, _____ you should go there.
6 The children found a magic box _____ they were at their friend's house.

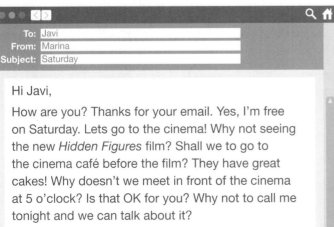

WHAT ARE THEY
READING?

1 Read the article about what students are reading. Who is reading something they are going to give back when they finish?

HOME   **NEWS**   **REVIEWS**   **RECOMMENDED**   **SHOP**

Last week we interviewed three students. We asked the question: *What are you reading today?* and we got some interesting answers.

Ethan likes action and adventure stories. He read *I am Number Four* by Pittacus Lore last summer because his parents gave it to him for his birthday. He loved it, so now he's reading the next book about the same characters, called *The Power of Six*. There are six books in total and they are about a group of young people with special powers. They come from another world. It's a fantastic book and a great story. Ethan wants to read the other four books, too.

Alyssa doesn't like reading books very much, but she loves bike magazines. She's a big fan of cycling. She loves riding and watching it on TV, so this week she's reading *Cycle Week*. It has all the information about new bikes and the important riders in the Tour de France. She doesn't buy the magazine because it's expensive, but her uncle lends it to her after he reads it.

Lily says, 'I read everything!' She gets one or two books a week from the library. She reads every night before she goes to sleep. At the moment she's reading *The Dragonfly Pool* by Eva Ibbotson. This is about a girl called Tally and her adventures in a country called Bergania. Lily thinks it's brilliant because it's about good fighting against bad. Can you guess who wins? You should read the book to find out!

2 Read the article again and answer the questions.

1 Where did Ethan get *I am Number Four* from?
2 Where do the people in Ethan's book come from?
3 What is Alyssa's favourite sport?
4 Why doesn't she buy *Cycle Week*?
5 When does Lily read books?
6 What is her opinion of the book, *The Dragonfly Pool*?

LISTENING

🔊 **1** Sofia calls a cinema and listens to a message.
Write the numbers Sofia needs to press (1–5) for
the information below. Which numbers does she
choose?

A to hear about the café ....
B to buy tickets ....
C to talk to an assistant ....
D to hear about next week's new film ....
E to hear about this week's new film ....

Sofia chooses numbers .... and
....

🔊 **2** Listen again and answer the questions.

1 What is the name of the cinema?
....

2 What is this week's film called?
....

3 How much are the tickets?
....

4 What is the name of the café?
....

5 What cakes can you buy in the café?
....
....

WRITING   A review

1 Read the review of a website. Does the writer like
it? Which words and phrases show how good or
bad it was? <u>Underline</u> them.

TeenInk – FOR THE BEST BOOKS

This website is great because teenagers write the reviews. Some of them are really interesting but others are boring. There are also reviews of films and music. Last week I wrote about a brilliant film called *Coco*. It's fun to see my own writing online! Why don't you try to write a review there, too?

2 Complete the table with the adjectives in the box.

> amazing   awful   boring   brilliant
> exciting   fantastic   great   horrible
> interesting   terrible

Good opinion	Bad opinion

3 Complete the sentences with the words in the box.

> boring   go   loved   should   sure

1 I .... it.
2 I think it is ....
3 Make .... you see it.
4 You .... go there.
5 .... and eat there.

4 Think about a website you like and answer the
questions.

1 What is it called?
....

2 What can you do on the website?
....

3 What is good about it?
....

4 What is not good about it?
....

5 What suggestion can you make about it?
....

5 Write your review. Use your answers to the
questions in Exercise 4 and write about 50 words.

....
....
....
....
....
....

19 SCHOOL CAN BE FUN!

VOCABULARY Trip activities

1 Match the verbs to the phrases to make school trip activities.

1 cook ....
2 dance ....
3 go ....
4 go on ....
5 visit ....
6 watch ....

a a nature walk
b an aquarium
c at a disco
d a show
e on a fire
f round a museum

2 Choose the correct words to complete the sentences.

1 We went *on / in* a long walk in the country last weekend.
2 It was fun dancing *on / at* the disco in the evening.
3 My friends and I had a good time at the amusement *ride / park* on my birthday.
4 We cooked fish *on / in* a fire in the camp.
5 Our class went *at / round* a museum to see the dinosaurs.
6 Their English teacher took them to watch a *show / farm* at the theatre.

3 Complete the sentences with the words in the box.

> amusement   aquarium
> disco   farm   fire   museum
> river   sailing   show   walk

1 We really enjoyed dancing at a .... on the last night of the camp.
2 I like going round the science .... because there are lots of interesting things to do.
3 The .... had a big collection of fish, including sharks!
4 I'd like to go .... on the sea in a big boat.
5 Last summer I went canoeing along a .... with a group of friends.
6 They cooked food on a .... and it was delicious.
7 My class is going on a nature .... to study the trees in the forest behind our school.
8 We went on a school trip to visit a .... to learn about looking after sheep and cows.
9 We all went to the theatre to watch a ....
10 At the end of term all the students in year 8 go to an .... park for the day.

GRAMMAR have to / don't have to

1 Look at the pictures and write sentences with the correct form of *have to* and the phrases.

There are lots of rules at our school ...

0 leave phones
We have to leave our phones at home.

1 be quiet

2 wear a uniform

3 start school

4 go to school

5 learn Spanish

2 Complete the sentences with the correct form of *have to*.

1 Andy _____ do any homework today because he finished it all yesterday.
2 Sonya can't go to the cinema tomorrow because she _____ look after her little brother.
3 We _____ go to school tomorrow because it's Sunday.
4 My brother _____ wear school uniform. He can wear jeans and a T-shirt to school.
5 I _____ catch the bus to school because I can't walk there. It's too far.
6 My mum and dad _____ go to work at the weekend. They can stay at home.

3 Choose the correct words to complete the sentences.

1 I *have / has* to do lots of homework for school.
2 You *has / have* to wear sports clothes.
3 *I've / I have* to buy a present for my sister.
4 It's warm here, but I think holidays *have / has* to be more interesting.
5 You *don't have / haven't* to bring anything.
6 *We've / We have* to bring a nature picture.

4 Complete the sentences with the correct form of *have to* or *can*.

1 The teacher didn't give us any homework today, so this afternoon I _____ go to the park because I _____ do anything for school.
2 In my school we _____ have lunch in the school dining room or we _____ go home to eat.
3 Nathan wears his own clothes to school. He _____ wear a uniform, but in Hannah's school the students _____ wear their own clothes because they _____ wear a uniform.

1 Match the sentence halves.

1 Mr Kelly, our history teacher, gives
2 Last term my class group had to do
3 My biology teacher talks so fast it's difficult to take
4 She didn't study so she
5 I didn't do any
6 I'm sure I'm going to pass
7 I don't like only studying from
8 My brother got very good

a a project about the sea in our natural science class.
b failed the test.
c marks in his final exams.
d really good lessons.
e the English test because I learned all the vocabulary.
f a textbook because I think we need the teacher's help, too.
g notes about everything she says.
h homework last night because I wasn't well.

2 Complete the text with the words in the box.

exercises   homework   lessons   marks
notes   projects   tests   textbooks

My school is great. The teachers give interesting [1] _____ and they give us a lot of help so we can pass our [2] _____ and exams. I always get good [3] _____ for the work we do in class! Sometimes we study from [4] _____ but often we do [5] _____ in class about interesting topics. Last week, a scientist came to our class to talk to us. We had to take [6] _____ and then make a poster about his talk. We often have to do [7] _____ after school and at weekends, but only a few [8] _____ for about an hour a day, so I have time for other activities.

School *is fun!*

1 Read the article about a school and tick (✓) the things the students can do there.

1 They can go swimming. ....
2 They can play basketball. ....
3 They can learn languages. ....
4 They can wear their own clothes. ....
5 They can have class outside. ....

My brother's school is called Summer Tree Academy. It's a very big school in a small town in Western Australia. It has 35 classrooms, a few libraries and two gyms. It also has a large swimming pool. The students love it. This school is very old. The first students went to Summer Tree Academy 100 years ago. Some of the buildings are very beautiful.

People go to the school when they're 12. They can leave when they're 16, or they can stay until they're 18. Students can study lots of different subjects. Everyone has to study English, maths and science, but they can choose drama, computer programming or photography. They don't have to study a language, but some students really enjoy learning Spanish and Chinese.

Students don't have to wear a uniform at Summer Tree Academy. They can wear what they like, but they can only wear shorts if it's very hot. Teachers at the school believe that students enjoy school more if they don't wear a uniform. My brother really enjoys going to Summer Tree Academy and my little sister can't wait to start at the school.

2 Read the article again. Are the sentences right (✓) or wrong (✗)?

1 Summer Tree Academy is a very small school. ....
2 The school has more than one library. ....
3 Summer Tree Academy is a new school. ....
4 Students can only leave the school when they are 18. ....
5 Students study photography if they want to. ....
6 All students at Summer Tree Academy study Chinese. ....
7 Teachers like the students to wear uniforms. ....
8 Boys and girls go to Summer Tree Academy. ....

🔊 19

✓ 1 You will hear a teacher telling his class about a school trip. For each question, write the correct answer in each gap. Write one word or a number or a date or a time.

School trip

Place: Ireland

Time of flight: ¹ _____

Things to bring for the journey: ² _____ and snacks

Clothes to take: comfortable clothes, trainers and a ³ _____

Saturday afternoon activity: ⁴ _____

Day of return to school: ⁵ _____

WRITING   A text about your perfect school

1 Read the text about Oliver's perfect school and tick (✓) the things he talks about.

1 places in the school   ....
2 what students can do   ....
3 the size of the school   ....
4 the school trips   ....
5 what the teachers are like   ....
6 the time students start school ....
7 what students have to do   ....
8 the age of the students   ....
9 the name of the school   ....

2 Think about your perfect school. Use some of the ideas in Exercise 1 and your own ideas. Make notes below.

_____
_____
_____
_____

3 Write about your perfect school. Use the notes you made in Exercise 2 and write about 50 words.

_____
_____
_____
_____
_____
_____

My perfect school – Oliver

My perfect school is called Best School. It's a big school. We can do sports and there's a swimming pool. There's also a nice restaurant with good food. The teachers are wonderful and students can study the subjects they like. I like science, so in my school we can do experiments and projects about nature. We don't have to do tests and the teachers don't give us any homework.

20 FAMILIES

VOCABULARY Family

1 Use the clues and the family tree to complete the crossword.

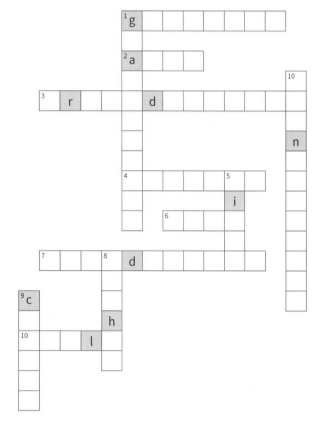

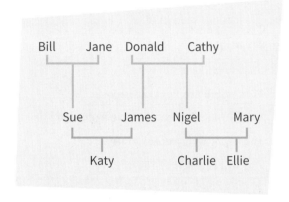

Bill Jane Donald Cathy

Sue James Nigel Mary

Katy Charlie Ellie

Across
1 Charlie is Cathy's …
2 Sue is Charlie's …
3 Katy is Jane's …
4 Nigel is Mary's …
6 Sue is James's …
7 Cathy is Ellie's …
10 James is Charlie's …

Down
1 Donald is Charlie's …
5 Katy is Mary's …
8 Charlie is Sue's …
9 Ellie is Katy's …
10 Bill and Jane are Katy's …

2 What family word do the letters in the grey boxes in Exercise 1 spell?

3 Put the letters in *italics* in the correct order to make adjectives to describe the people.

4 Complete the sentences with words in Exercise 3.
1 My sister has got _____ hair. She isn't blonde.
2 My mother isn't fat. She's _____.
3 His brother is _____. He's only three years old.
4 She's 1.90 m. That's very _____!
5 He's very _____. He's only 1.10 m.

My grandmother is very ¹ *lod* now. When she was ² *nguoy* she was very ³ *tibuleafu*. She had ⁴ *rakd* hair and brown eyes and she was ⁵ *msil*. My grandfather was very ⁶ *odgo-onlikgo* too but he was ⁷ *ifra* with blue eyes. He was very ⁸ *altl*, about 1.80 m. My mother is like my grandfather. She is ⁹ *etrpyt* and has ¹⁰ *olnbed* hair. The difference is that she is ¹¹ *rosht* and she has brown eyes.

GRAMMAR Adverbs of manner

1 Look at the adjectives and write the adverbs.

1 bad
2 noisy
3 hard
4 careful
5 quick
6 happy
7 easy
8 good
9 fast
10 quiet

2 Complete the sentences with the words in the box.

badly	fast	hard
loudly	slowly	well

1 I worked really _____ on my history project all weekend.
2 My brother isn't very happy. He did _____ in his exams last week.
3 I can't run very _____. I think I'm the slowest in my class.
4 Don't talk so _____, Josh. We have to be quiet in the library.
5 I didn't do very _____ in my chemistry test. My teacher wants me to do it again.
6 Come on! Hurry up! Why are you walking so _____?

3 Correct the mistakes in the sentences.

👁 1 We study together very happy.
2 Be carefully with the dog.
3 The team was playing very bad.
4 You can find my house very easy.
5 It was my favourite match because both teams played very good.
6 I liked it a lot because the players played wonderful.

4 Complete the sentences with adverbs made from the correct adjectives in brackets.

1 Sophie ran _____ to the bus stop because she was late. (slow / quick)
2 Liam is in the school orchestra because he plays the violin _____. (good / bad)
3 Think _____ before you choose the answer. (careful / noisy)
4 My sister was singing _____ in the shower because she was going to a party. (happy / sad)
5 He did his homework _____ and got a very low mark. (good / bad)
6 Please speak _____ so everyone can hear you. (wonderful / loud)

VOCABULARY Adverbs of degree

1 Choose the correct words to complete the sentences.

1 **A:** What shall we get Dana for her birthday?
   B: She likes reading, so she'd *probably / nearly* like a book.
2 **A:** What was the film like?
   B: Well, it wasn't the best film, but it was *quite / really* good, I suppose.
3 **A:** Do you like the computer game?
   B: Yes! It's *quite / really* good!
4 **A:** What do you think of our new music teacher?
   B: I *really / nearly* like him.
5 **A:** Tom did well in his exams, didn't he?
   B: Yes, he *certainly / almost* worked hard.
6 **A:** What time will we get there?
   B: Very soon, don't worry. We're *quite / nearly* there.

2 Complete the sentences with the words in the box.

certainly	nearly	probably
quite	really	

1 My sister _____ likes playing tennis. She plays every day.
2 Alisha's _____ going to win the race, I'm sure. She's the fastest runner in the class.
3 He's _____ 15 years old. His birthday is next week.
4 I did _____ well in my chemistry test. I got 80%.
5 I'm not sure but I think I _____ left my book at home.

1 For each question, write the correct answer. Write one word for each gap.

My big sister

by Lauren Taylor

My older sister's name [0] *is* Yolanda. She's tall and slim with long, dark hair. She's five years older [1] _____ me and I think she's [2] _____ best sister in the world. I haven't got any other brothers or sisters. We live in a little house with [3] _____ parents in a town near the mountains. She goes to university in the city, so she has [4] _____ take the bus every day to go to class. She wants to be a teacher [5] _____ she leaves university. I think she's going to be a good teacher [6] _____ she loves children.

2 Read about the rest of Lauren's family and answer the questions below.

Our family

Our family is quite small but we spend a lot of time together. We really like going on holiday to different places. We usually go to a hotel near the beach or in the mountains. We often go for long walks. My dad is teaching me and my sister to climb. It's awesome! At the weekends we sometimes go to the cinema. Yolanda has to study a lot, but she always has time to help me with my homework. My dad is a teacher, so he can help my sister with her studies. I want to be an engineer, like my mum. She's very good at numbers and can explain everything about maths. I like cooking, so I make pasta for all the family when they're busy!

1 Where do the family like going on holiday?

2 What is Lauren's father teaching his children?

3 How does Yolanda help her sister?

4 What is Lauren's mum's job?

5 How does Lauren help her family?

LISTENING

1 Listen to Mason talking about his family. Which day of the week do all the family eat together?

....

2 Listen again and match the family words to the names.

1 mother ....
2 father ....
3 older sister ....
4 younger sister ....
5 grandmother ....
6 uncle ....

a Anita
b Natalie
c Katie
d George
e Matthew
f Sam

3 Listen again. Are the sentences right (✓) or wrong (✗)?

1 Mason's mother sometimes works at the weekend. ....
2 Mason's father works in an office. ....
3 Natalie's dance class is on Saturday mornings. ....
4 Katie is a good student. ....
5 Anita likes going out in the evening. ....
6 George is 44 years old. ....

WRITING — A description of a family member

1 Choose the correct words to complete Maria's description of her cousin.

My favourite cousin

My cousin James is nearly 24 years old, almost 10 years older ¹ *than / that* me. He lives in Manchester. He works ² *in / on* a bank. I think he's very good-looking ³ *so / because* he's tall with quite long hair and beautiful brown eyes. He's also a musician. He plays the guitar in a band. He's really funny and always spends time with ⁴ *my / me* when he comes to visit us. I ⁵ *doesn't / don't* often see him, because he's very busy.

2 Put the words in the correct order to make sentences.

1 aunt / near / house / my / quite / lives / my

....

2 really / has / long / got / she / hair

....

3 mother / is / she / almost / as / as / my / old

....

4 enjoy / I / certainly / her / seeing

....

3 Think of a person who doesn't live with you, like a cousin, uncle or aunt. Make notes about what he / she does, what he / she looks like and what you like about him / her.

....
....
....
....
....

4 Write about your family member. Use the notes you made in Exercise 3 and write about 50 words.

....
....
....
....
....
....
....

Acknowledgements

The authors and publishers acknowledge the following sources of copyright material and are grateful for the permissions granted. While every effort has been made, it has not always been possible to identify the sources of all the material used, or to trace all copyright holders. If any omissions are brought to our notice, we will be happy to include the appropriate acknowledgements on reprinting and in the next update to the digital edition, as applicable.

Key: U = Unit, SU = Starter Unit.

Text
U3: Sylvia Young Theatre School for the text about Sylvia Young Theatre School. Copyright © Sylvia Young Theatre School. Reproduced with kind permission.

Photography
The following images are sourced from Getty Images.

SU: Wittayayut/iStock/Getty Images Plus; Gosia Schamel/EyeEm; kreinick/iStock/Getty Images Plus; Alex Potemkin/iStock/Getty Images Plus; asiseeit/E+; **U1:** Klaus Vedfelt/DigitalVision; Nicola Tree/Taxi gbh007/iStock/Getty Images Plus; vm/E+; Zengineer/iStock/Getty Images Plus; Pilin_Petunyia/iStock/Getty Images Plus; Dennis Welsh/UpperCut Images; John Lund/Blend Images; Kelly Funk/All Canada Photos; rbv/iStock/Getty Images Plus; Jose Luis Pelaez Inc/Blend Images; Mikael Vaisanen/Corbis; Delpixart/iStock Editorial/Getty Images Plus; Kittiyut Phornphibul /EyeEm; Thomas Barwick/Taxi; **U2:** Atli Mar Hafsteinsson/Cultura; Christine Schneider/Cultura; vitranc/E+; Richard Drury/DigitalVision; VOISIN/PHANIE/Passage; Tetra Images; stocknroll/iStock / Getty Images Plus andresr/E+; Hero Images; Peter Muller/Cultura; Thinkstock/Stockbyte; gjohnstonphoto/iStock/Getty Images Plus; JacobVanHouten/E+; papkin/iStock/Getty Images Plus; kiko_jimenez/iStock/Getty Images Plus; fstop123/E+; Westend61; Indeed; **U3:** mevans/iStock/Getty Images Plus; PhotoGraphyKM/iStock/Getty Images Plus; Hein von Horsten/Gallo Images; Stockbyte; Fred Choi/EyeEm; golubovy/iStock/Getty Images Plus; skynesher/E+; Keipher McKennie/Getty Images Entertainment; **U4:** Niedring/Drentwett/MITO images; Plan Shoot/Multi-bits/The Image Bank; Steve_Gadomski/iStock/Getty Images Plus; ewg3D/E+; Christopher Polk/Billboard Awards 2014/Getty Images Entertainment; **U5:** Highwaystarz-Photography/iStock/Getty Images Plus; Dave Porter Peterborough Uk./VisitBritain; Pierre-Yves Babelon/Moment; Peter Adams/Taxi; Jose A. Bernat Bacete/Moment; Radu Razvan Gheorghe/EyeEm; Photo 12/Universal Images Group; Bettmann; Library of Congress/Corbis Historical/VCG; Garry Gay/Photolibrary; Sovfoto/Universal Images Group; Imagno/Hulton Fine Art Collection; Art Rickerby/The LIFE Picture Collection; skynesher/E+; calvindexter/DigitalVision Vectors; **U6:** Morsa Images/Taxi; Klaus Vedfelt/Iconica; Ben Welsh/Corbis; Hero Images; Wavebreakmedia/iStock/Getty Images Plus; Monty Rakusen/Cultura; South_agency/E+; Digital Vision./Photodisc; Soundsnaps/iStock/Getty Images Plus; George Doyle/Stockbyte; Jose Luis Pelaez Inc./Blend Images; Juanmonino/E+; Comstock/Stockbyte; **U7:** VisitBritain/Rod Edwards; Itziar Aio/Moment; Martin Sundberg/UpperCut Images; PamelaJoeMcFarlane/E+; ROMAOSLO/E+; Ben Gingell/iStock/Getty Images Plus; Plush Studios/Bill Reitzel/Blend Images; Zave Smith/Image Source; alxpin/E+; Fine Art Images/Heritage Images/Hulton Archive; DEA/G. DAGLI ORTI/De Agostini; Martin Child/DigitalVision; **U8:** Noi_Pattanan/iStock/Getty Images Plus; Emya/iStock/Getty Images Plus; Steven Taylor/Photonica; Daniel Sambraus/EyeEm; Dougal Waters/Photodisc; Rick Lew/DigitalVision; lisa kimberly/Moment Open; Tavia/Moment; George Doyle/Stockbyt; Merisa I Mesi/EyeEm; Spiderstock/E+; Comstock/Stockbyte; Antonel/iStock/Getty Images Plus; **U9:** KhongkitWiriyachan/iStock/Getty Images Plus; Suparat Malipoom/EyeEm; C Squared Studios/Photodisc; pic_studio/iStock/Getty Images Plus; Chee Siong Teh/EyeEm; Serg_Velusceac/iStock/Getty Images Plus; sankai/iStock/Getty Images Plus; Creative Crop/Photodisc; BSANI/iStock/Getty Images Plus; Shana Novak/DigitalVision; subjug/iStock/Getty Images Plus; Tom Kolossa/EyeEm; Amir Mukhtar/Moment; Chris Ryan/OJO Images; Ryan McVay/DigitalVision; Glowimages; Westend61; **U10:** drbimages/iStock/Getty Images Plus; Klaus Tiedge/Corbis; Atlantide Phototravel/Corbis Documentary; William Manning/Corbis Documentary; Ian Cumming/Perspectives; Juanmonino/E+; **U11:** Pnuar006/iStock/Getty Images Plus; Keith Bedford/The Boston Globe; Carsten Schanter/EyeEm; Stockbyte; Compassionate Eye Foundation/Robert Kent/DigitalVision; japatino/Moment Open; **U12:** Ivary; LordRunar/E+; George Doyle & Ciaran Griffin/Stockbyte; stockcam/E+; Paper Boat Creative/Photodisc; ET-ARTWORKS/DigitalVision Vectors; pagadesign/E+; lvcandy/DigitalVision Vectors; Olly Curtis/T3 Magazine/Future; luismmolina/E+; s-cphoto/E+; mbortolino/E+; Olivier Morin/AFP; VI-Images/Getty Images Sport; Mehmet Kaman/Anadolu Agency; FatCamera/E+; John Eder/The Image Bank; **U13:** philipimage/iStock/Getty Images Plus; FS Productions/Blend Images; drbimages/E+; Hinterhaus Productions/DigitalVision; Sigrid Gombert/Cultura; Yasser Chalid/Moment; Layland Masuda/Moment Open; Vesnaandjic/E+; Tim Kitchen/The Image Bank; Westend61; abezikus/iStock/Getty Images Plus; Rolf Bruderer/Blend Images; clubfoto/E+; Martine Hamilton Knight/ArcaidImages/Arcaid Images; Shalom Ormsby/Blend Images; **U14:** Universal History Archive/Universal Images Group; Zsolt Hlinka/Moment; Gavin Hellier; Davide Seddio/Moment; **U15:** Leland Bobbe/Image Source; Martin Farkas/EyeEm; aleks1949/iStock/Getty Images Plus; **U16:** annick vanderschelden photography/Moment; Vicki Jauron, Babylon and Beyond Photography/Moment; Tim Oram/Oxford Scientific; Delta Images/Cultura; Rijanti Wijaya/EyeEm; Jose Lodos Benavente/iStock / Getty Images Plus; CreativeNature_nl/iStock/Getty Images Plus; Mick Hickman/EyeEm; Tony Emmett/Moment; Thinkstock Images/Stockbyte; Westend61; CraigRJD/iStock/Getty Images Plus; **U17:** Beck Photography; Tetra Images; John Patrick Fletcher/Action Plus; Westend61; Peter Dazeley/The; Image Bank; simonkr/E+; Richard Wareham/Photolibrary; Simon James/GC Images; **U18:** AndreyPopov/iStock/Getty Images Plus; simonkr/E+; Alexander Spatari/Moment; g-stockstudio/iStock/Getty Images Plus; Kate Sheppard/Ikon Images; monkeybusinessimages/iStock/Getty Images Plus; Compassionate Eye Foundation/joSon/Photodisc; Steve Debenport/E+; Brad Wilson/Stone; **U19:** Portra/DigitalVision, kokkai/iStock/Getty Images Plus; Ulrike Schmitt-Hartmann/DigitalVision; Bloom Productions/Taxi; Hero Images; **U20:** H. Armstrong Roberts/Retrofile RF; Hill Street Studios/Blend Images; Hero Images; KidStock/Blend Images; Alex Tihonovs/EyeEm, no_limit_pictures/iStock Unreleased.

The following photographs have been sourced from other library/sources.

U12: Courtesy of University of Michigan.

Front cover photography by wacomka/iStock/Getty Images Plus.

Illustration
Humberto Blanco (Sylvie Poggio Artists Agency); Richard Jones (Beehive Illustration), Nigel Dobbyn (Beehive Illustration), Amerigo Pinelli (Advocate Art).

URLS
The publisher has made every effort to ensure that the URLs for external websites referred to in this book are correct and active at the time of printing. However, the publisher takes no responsibility for the websites and can make no guarantees that sites will remain live or that their content is or will remain appropriate.

The publishers are grateful to the following contributors: cover design and design concept: restless; typesetting: emc design Ltd; audio recordings: produced by Leon Chambers and recorded at The SoundHouse Studios, London; project management: Louise Davoren